WILLS AND ESTATE PLANNING HANDBOOK FOR OREGON

WILLS AND ESTATE PLANNING HANDBOOK FOR OREGON

Rees C. Johnson, Attorney

Self-Counsel Press Inc.
a subsidiary of
International Self-Counsel Press Ltd.
Canada   U.S.A.
(Printed in Canada)

Copyright © 1978, 1996 by Self-Counsel Press Inc.

All rights reserved. No part of this book may be reproduced or transmitted in any form by any means — graphic, electronic, or mechanical — without permission in writing from the publisher, except by a reviewer who may quote brief passages in a review.

Printed in Canada

First edition: May, 1978
Second edition: July, 1983
Third edition: November, 1987
Fourth edition: June, 1990
Fifth edition: February, 1996

Cataloguing in Publication Data

Johnson, Rees C., 1938-
    Wills and estate planning handbook for Oregon

(Self-counsel legal series)
ISBN 1-55180-054-3

1. Wills — Oregon — Popular works. 2. Estate planning — Oregon — Popular works. 3. Probate law and practice — Oregon — Popular works. I. Title II. Series.
KF02544.Z9J65 1995   346.79808'4   C95-910872-6

Cover photography by Terry Guscott, ATN Visuals, Vancouver, B.C.

Self-Counsel Press Inc.
a subsidiary of
International Self-Counsel Press Ltd.
Head and Editorial Office
1481 Charlotte Road
North Vancouver, British Columbia V7J 1H1

U.S. Address
1704 N. State Street
Bellingham, Washington 98225

CONTENTS

	PREFACE	xvii
1	**INTRODUCTION**	1
	a. What is estate planning?	1
	b. The estate planning process	2
	1. What do you own?	2
	2. Who are the beneficiaries?	3
	3. Set your goals	3
	4. Implement your goals	3
	5. Review your plans	3
2	**THE MEANING OF PROBATE AND NONPROBATE**	4
	a. What the words mean	4
	1. Estate	4
	2. Real and personal property	5
	3. Probate and nonprobate property	5
	4. Probate administration	5
	5. Will	6
	6. Intestate succession	6
	b. The differences between probate and nonprobate property	7
	c. Some property can be either probate or nonprobate	8
	1. Life insurance	8
	2. Other contract property	9
	3. Businesses	9
	4. Property without documents of title	11

3 PROBATE PROPERTY — 12
  a. Sole ownership — 12
  b. Tenancy in common — 12
  1. Inheritances and devises — 13
  2. Personal property owned by spouses — 13
  3. Real property owned by divorced spouses — 14
  4. Invalid marriage — 15
  5. What you should know about a tenancy in common — 15
  c. Remainder interest — 17
  d. Inheritance, devise, or trust distribution — 18
  e. Other probate property — 18
  f. Community property — 19

4 NONPROBATE PROPERTY — 21
  a. Tenancy by the entirety — 22
  b. Other survivorship — real property — 22
  c. Survivorship — personal property — 23
  d. Seller-financed real property sales — 23
  e. U.S. government securities — 24
  f. Life estates and remainders — 25
  g. Joint bank accounts — 27
  1. Features of joint accounts — 27
  2. Changes in law for joint accounts — 29
  3. Avoiding joint account problems — 30
  h. Living trusts and POD property — 31

5 INTRODUCTION TO TRUSTS — 34
  a. Trustor, trustee, and beneficiary — 34
  b. Categories of trusts — 35
  c. Anatomy of a trust — 35

	d.	Revocable living trust	37
		1. Funded revocable living trust	38
		2. The standby living trust	38
		3. The self-declaration of trust	39
		4. The revocable life insurance trust	39
	e.	Irrevocable living trusts	40
		1. Irrevocable life insurance trusts	40
		2. Charitable remainder trusts	40
	f.	Testamentary trusts	41
	g.	Trusts and tax savings	42
	h.	The duties of a trustee	42
	i.	How to select a trustee	43
		1. Professional management	43
		2. Impartiality	44
		3. Perpetual existence	44
		4. Dishonesty	44
		5. Trustee's fee	45
	j.	Your rights as a beneficiary	45
6	**THE FUNDED REVOCABLE LIVING TRUST**		**47**
	a.	Introduction	47
	b.	The trust documents	47
	c.	Living trusts for married couples	49
		1. The joint and survivorship living trust	49
		2. The common joint living trust	50
		3. The community property joint living trust	50
		4. Separate trusts for each spouse	50
	d.	Funding the trust	50
		1. General funding rules	51
		2. Real property	52

		3.	Other assets	54
	e.	Tax aspects of living trusts		54
		1.	Income taxes	54
		2.	Gift taxes	55
		3.	Death taxes	55
	f.	Periodic review		56
	g.	Settlement at trustor's death		57
	h.	The pros and cons		57
7	**WHAT HAPPENS WHEN YOU DIE WITHOUT A WILL?**			61
	a.	Introduction		61
	b.	Who are your heirs?		62
		1.	Heirs and devisees	62
		2.	Surviving spouse	62
		3.	Issue and lineal descendants	64
		4.	Representation	64
	c.	Who gets what?		65
	d.	Special rules governing heirs		66
		1.	Afterborn heirs	66
		2.	Survivorship by 120 hours	66
		3.	Persons of the half blood	66
		4.	Adopted children	66
		5.	Unmarried parents	68
	e.	Other costs of neglect		68
8	**ALL ABOUT WILLS**			70
	a.	What the words mean		70
	b.	What is a will?		71
	c.	What makes a will valid?		72
		1.	Age requirement	72

	2.	Mental capacity	72
	3.	Undue influence	74
d.	Signing your will		77
	1.	Read the will	77
	2.	Take your time	77
	3.	Stay calm and alert	78
	4.	Objective witnesses	78
	5.	The formal requirements	78
e.	How a will is revoked		82
	1.	Marriage	82
	2.	By annulment or divorce	83
	3.	By a new will	84
	4.	By destruction	84
f.	Agreements concerning wills		85
g.	Wills signed in other states		86
h.	Where to keep your will		87
	1.	Safe deposit box	87
	2.	Trust department	87
	3.	At home	87
	4.	Attorney's office	87
	5.	With other people	88
i.	Letter of instructions		89
j.	Review your will and estate plan		90
k.	Safe deposit boxes		91
	1.	Reasonable basis	91
	2.	Attorney	92
	3.	Personal representative	92

9	**PLANNING YOUR WILL**	**93**
	a. The opening clause	94
	b. Your heirs	95
	c. Personal representative	97
	d. When you own real property in another state	99
	e. How to make gifts in your will	100
	1. Specific devise	100
	2. General devise	100
	3. Residue	100
	f. Planning specific and general devises	101
	g. What if property is sold or destroyed?	102
	1. Insured property	102
	2. Sale of property	103
	3. Condemnation	103
	4. Stocks and bonds	103
	h. Mortgages and other encumbrances	104
	i. Who pays the bills?	104
	j. Who pays death taxes?	106
	k. Who gets the income during probate?	107
	l. Your tangible personal property	107
	m. What if a devisee dies before you do?	109
	n. Survivorship	110
	o. Guardian	111
10	**SIMULTANEOUS DEATHS, SLAYERS, AND DISCLAIMERS**	**113**
	a. Simultaneous deaths	113
	b. Slayers	114
	1. Probate property	115
	2. Joint and survivorship property	115

		3. Life estates and remainders	116
		4. Life insurance	116
	c.	Disclaimers	116
11	**MARRIAGE AND WILLS**		119
	a.	Property rights of spouses	119
		1. Divorce	119
		2. Death	119
	b.	Marital property agreements	121
		1. Premarital agreements	121
		2. Postnuptial agreements	122
		3. Different kinds of agreements	122
	c.	Agreements for unmarried couples	124
	d.	Are you really married?	125
12	**GIFTS TO MINORS**		127
	a.	What is a minor?	127
	b.	Minors and the law	127
	c.	Custodianships	128
		1. How to set up a custodianship	128
		2. Who can be a custodian?	128
		3. Duties and powers of the custodian	129
		4. Court supervision	129
		5. Expenses and compensation	130
		6. Ending the custodianship	130
		7. Income taxes	130
	d.	Conservatorships	131
		1. How to set up a conservatorship	131
		2. Who can be a conservator?	131
		3. Duties and powers of a conservator	132
		4. Court supervision	132

	5.	Expenses	133
	6.	Ending a conservatorship	133
	7.	Incapacity	133
	8.	Multiple conservatorships	134
e.	Trusts		134
	1.	How to set up a trust for a minor	134
	2.	Who can be a trustee?	134
	3.	Duties and powers	134
	4.	Court supervision	135
	5.	Expenses	135
	6.	Ending a trust	135
	7.	Incapacity	135
	8.	Multiple trusts or beneficiaries	135
f.	Guardianships		136
	1.	Setting up a guardianship	136
	2.	Who can be a guardian?	136
	3.	Duties of a guardian	136
g.	Revocable trust accounts and other POD accounts for minors		137

13 PLANNING FOR INCAPACITY — 139

a. Health care decisions — 139
b. New health care forms — 139
    1. The advance directive — 140
    2. Signing the advance directive — 140
    3. Distributing the advance directive — 145
    4. Making decisions for you — 145
    5. Former health care documents — 145
    6. Mental health declaration — 146
c. Property and financial decisions — 146

		1.	Conservatorships and guardianships	146
		2.	Power of attorney	147
		3.	Revocable living trust	148
		4.	Joint bank accounts	148
	d.		Long-term health care	149
14	**ANATOMICAL GIFTS**			153
	a.		Who may be a donor?	153
	b.		How to make the gift	154
		1.	Sign a donor card	154
		2.	Sign a form at the Motor Vehicle Division	154
		3.	Make the gift in your will	155
		4.	Make the gift in your advance directive	155
	c.		How to amend or revoke the gift	155
	d.		Duties of procurement organization	156
15	**PROBATE ADMINISTRATION**			157
	a.		Locating the will	157
	b.		Who handles the probate?	158
	c.		How to start probate proceedings	159
	d.		Personal representative's bond	160
	e.		Court appointment of the personal representative	160
	f.		Notice to heirs and devisees	160
	g.		Notifying interested persons	161
	h.		Listing the property	162
	i.		What the personal representative does	162
	j.		Claims against the estate	163
	k.		What happens when probate is delayed?	165
	l.		Final account	165

	m.	Paying the personal representative and attorneys	167
	n.	Rights of the spouse and dependent children during probate	167
	o.	What the surviving spouse is entitled to	168
	p.	Liabilities of a personal representative	169
	q.	Will contests	170
16	**WHEN YOU LEAVE A SMALL ESTATE**		171
	a.	The small estate affidavit	171
		1. Qualifying property	171
		2. The affidavit	171
	b.	Deposits with financial institutions	174
	c.	Motor vehicles	175
	d.	Wages	175
	e.	Unpaid money	175
	f.	Real property	176
	g.	Savings bonds	176
	h.	Other assets	177
17	**ESTATE AND INHERITANCE TAXES**		178
	a.	The federal estate tax	178
		1. The gross estate	180
		2. Probate property	180
		3. Joint and survivorship property	181
		4. Property transferred before death	182
		5. Other nonprobate property	182
	b.	Deductions	183
	c.	Calculating the tax	183
	d.	Filing the return and paying the tax	185

		e.	The Oregon inheritance tax	185
		f.	Generation-skipping transfer tax	185
18	**GIFT TAXES DURING YOUR LIFETIME**			188
	a.		The federal gift tax	188
		1.	Kinds of gifts	188
		2.	Reporting gifts	189
	b.		The Oregon gift tax	190
	APPENDIX			191
	GLOSSARY			193

SAMPLES

#1	Certification of trust	53
#2	A simple will	80
#3	The advance directive	141

TABLES

#1	Unified rate schedule	186
#2	Maximum credit for state death taxes	187

NOTICE TO READERS

Laws are constantly changing. Every effort is made to keep this publication as current as possible. However, the author, the publisher, and the vendor make no representation or warranties regarding the outcome or the use to which the information in this book is put and are not assuming any liability for any claims, losses, or damages arising out of the use of this book. The reader should not rely on the author or publisher of this book for any professional advice. Please be sure you have the most recent edition.

Note: The fees quoted in this book are correct at the date of publication. However, fees are subject to change without notice. For current fees, check with the appropriate court or government office nearest you.

PREFACE

One of the major developments since the last edition of this book is the new popularity of the funded revocable living trust as the centerpiece of many estate plans. To explain this phenomenon, this edition contains a new chapter on the living trusts. (See chapter 6.)

This edition also reflects numerous changes in both federal and Oregon law since 1990.

Oregon has enacted a law defining an unmarried survivor of a deceased person as a "surviving spouse" for the limited purpose of inheriting a share of the deceased person's estate if the person dies without a will. The eligibility requirements are discussed in chapter 7.

Oregon has two new health care forms: the advance directive and the declaration for mental health treatment. Chapter 13 has been rewritten to describe these two new forms.

The federal Medicaid eligibility rules have changed (see chapter 13) and limits on the small estate affidavit have increased (see chapter 16).

The rules on anatomical gifts have changed and chapter 14 has been rewritten to reflect those changes.

Author's Newsletter for Oregon Residents

At least once a year, the author produces for his estate planning clients a newsletter about changes to the law concerning wills, trusts, probate, and death taxes as they apply to Oregon residents. The newsletter also serves as an update to this book and is available free of charge. To receive the newsletter, write to the author at the address below:

575 Lloyd Center Tower
825 N.E. Multnomah Street
Portland, Oregon 97232

Tel: (503) 232-3171

1
INTRODUCTION

The primary purpose of this book is to provide you with a practical guide to planning and writing your will or living trust. It cannot and does not attempt to replace professionals like lawyers and accountants who specialize in estate planning, but it should give you a general understanding of estate planning and the legal context in which it operates. It makes it easier for you to deal with and understand the professional advisors when you do seek their help. This book also clears up a number of common misconceptions about estate planning and helps you avoid making drastic mistakes.

a. WHAT IS ESTATE PLANNING?

To many people, estate planning means nothing more than having a will. They incorrectly assume that a will is all that is necessary to get their financial affairs in order, and that once it is signed they can file it away and forget about it.

While a will is central to many estates, for many individuals, a living trust has become the central document. Signing the documents, however, is merely one step in a process that starts with an analysis of your property and debts. This process may involve assistance from a number of different professional advisors, including a lawyer, an accountant, a trust officer, a life insurance agent, and an investment counselor.

Good estate planning means not only planning ahead so your affairs are in order when you die, but also planning today so that you can enjoy the maximum benefits from your property while you are alive.

Each estate plan should achieve the following goals:

(a) Preserve and build your wealth while you are alive and ensure financial security for yourself and your dependents

(b) Maintain control of your property and affairs while you are alive

(c) Minimize the cost and delay of the transfer to your intended beneficiaries

(d) Minimize taxes, both while you are alive (income and gift taxes), and at your death (estate and inheritance taxes)

A poor estate plan can shrink the value of your assets and create unnecessary taxes, attorney fees, and delay. A good estate plan will prevent the transfer of your property and wealth to "laughing heirs," that is, distant relatives you never met or knew during your lifetime.

b. THE ESTATE PLANNING PROCESS

A well-planned estate should be periodically reviewed and revised whenever there are changes in your circumstances, in your wealth, or in the law.

1. What do you own?

The first step is to make a list of all your property and debts. Include anything of value. You should try to value each item at current fair market value. This helps you estimate your taxes and income under various conditions.

You should also examine and assemble documents concerning property ownership, including deeds, mortgages, life insurance policies, and retirement programs.

2. Who are the beneficiaries?

The second step is to analyze your present state of affairs. If you have a will, check to see what property will pass under it and what will not. Check your life insurance policies to see who the beneficiaries are. You may discover that your estranged mother is the primary beneficiary, even though you have been married for 15 years and expect everything to go to your spouse. Or, if you are divorced, your ex-spouse may still hold title to some of your assets.

3. Set your goals

Once you are sure that you know where you are, the next step is to set your goals. Make sure that you are getting maximum return on your investments at minimum tax cost. This includes providing for sufficient cash funds to meet expenses at your death so that your property does not have to be sold at distress prices. Also make sure that your property will go to the intended beneficiaries and that steps are taken to minimize taxes.

4. Implement your goals

You already know that if you don't have a will, you need one. But you may also decide to change one or more of your investments, restructure ownership of certain assets, sign a trust agreement, or buy more life insurance. You might want to change beneficiaries, sign an advance directive, or make some lifetime gifts. These estate planning techniques are discussed more fully later in this book.

5. Review your plans

It is a good idea to schedule a periodic review of your plans. Take a regular financial inventory and review all your documents to make certain that they still reflect your goals. You might make an annual review on December 31 or on your birthday.

2
THE MEANING OF PROBATE AND NONPROBATE

To understand the role of a will or living trust and the function of probate procedure in estate planning, you must first understand the variety of ways in which property can be owned in Oregon and the significance of classifying property as probate or nonprobate.

This chapter defines some basic terms relating to estate planning and explains the difference between probate and nonprobate property. The next two chapters describe the ways you can own property in Oregon and how that property is transferred at death.

a. WHAT THE WORDS MEAN

1. Estate

Your estate consists of all your property, both real and personal, including land, houses, furniture, personal belongings, checking and savings accounts, business interests, investments, life insurance, retirement benefits, and anything else you own of value.

It includes not only property you own and in which you have all the interest, such as fee title to real property, but also property in which you have a part interest because you own it jointly with someone else (e.g., property held jointly with right of survivorship), or property in which you have a limited interest, such as a life estate. All of these together constitute your estate.

2. Real and personal property

You may own both real and personal property. Real property is land and generally includes buildings and other fixtures that are permanent parts of the land.

Personal property includes everything else and can be put into two categories: tangible personal property, such as furniture, clothing, and motor vehicles, and intangible personal property, such as stocks, bonds, bank accounts, life insurance, and contract rights.

3. Probate and nonprobate property

Your estate may consist of two types of property. The first type is property that is subject to probate administration. A good example is property in your own name, such as your home or other real property you own in fee title. Such property passes under your will and is subject to probate administration.

The other category of property is nonprobate property. Such property does not pass to another person under your will, and it is not subject to probate administration, either because your interest in it terminates on the date of your death and, therefore, there is nothing for you to give away, or because the property passes to some other designated person by law or by contract.

Common examples of nonprobate property are stocks and bonds that you own jointly with another person with right of survivorship and life insurance on your life in which you designate the beneficiary as some person rather than your estate. Property which is in a living trust at your death is another example of nonprobate property.

4. Probate administration

Probate administration is a court-supervised procedure for transferring your probate property upon your death from your name to the persons who are legally entitled to it either under the terms of your will or according to Oregon law.

It involves appointing a personal representative who is responsible for collecting all the property, paying all your creditors, paying expenses of administration, paying any taxes due, and distributing the property to the persons who are legally entitled to it.

The word "probate" generally refers to the manner in which a will's validity is established after someone has died. Administration of a deceased's estate generally refers to the court-supervised procedure for transferring the property, whether or not there is a will. For simplicity, the court procedure is described in this book as probate administration. Probate administration deals only with probate property. Nonprobate property is not subject to probate administration.

5. Will

A will is a legal document declaring your intentions concerning the disposition of your probate property after death. A will has no legal effect until it is admitted to probate (i.e., until its validity has been proven by proper court proceedings after the person making the will has died).

Most important, a will deals only with probate property. This does not mean that when you prepare your will you should ignore nonprobate property. For instance, if you own property jointly with right of survivorship, and you die first, the property will pass by law to the joint survivor and will not be subject to the terms of your will. However, if the other joint owner dies before you do, then that nonprobate property becomes probate property. This possibility should be planned for and covered by your will.

The person making the will is known as the testator (if male) or testatrix (if female). He or she is described as dying testate (i.e., with a will).

6. Intestate succession

A person who dies without a will is described as dying intestate. If you have probate property, it will be subject to probate administration regardless of whether or not you have a will.

If you do not have a will, the court will appoint a personal representative, and your property will pass to those persons whom the law has designated (see chapter 7). This law is called the law of intestate succession. It applies if you have no will or if, as sometimes happens, your will does not dispose of all your probate property.

b. THE DIFFERENCES BETWEEN PROBATE AND NONPROBATE PROPERTY

In Oregon there are two basic procedures for transferring ownership of property at death: probate and nonprobate. The procedure used depends on title or ownership of property at death. This rule is central to an understanding of estate planning in Oregon and to everything that follows in this book.

Probate property must go through probate in order to transfer ownership to the persons entitled to it. On the other hand, title to nonprobate property generally can be easily cleared when an owner dies. For example, assume that Michael died owning 250 shares of stock in a major national company. He owned 100 shares in his own name (a form of probate property) and 150 shares in joint survivor ownership with his sister, Mary (a form of nonprobate property). His will left his entire estate to his brother, John. In order for John to get the 100 shares that are to go to him, he would have to go through the probate procedure described later. Mary, on the other hand, would simply have to submit a few documents to a stock transfer agent to get the jointly owned 150 shares into her name alone.

If you die owning both probate and nonprobate property, your probate property must go through probate, but your nonprobate property does not. If you have a will, it determines who gets your probate property; if you do not have a will, Oregon's laws on intestate succession determine who gets your probate property.

If you have a will, however, it may dispose *only* of probate property and cannot determine who gets your nonprobate property. The manner in which you structure ownership of nonprobate property while you are alive will determine who receives that property. This occurs even if your will states something different. Also, a will cannot change probate property into nonprobate property.

If you die with only nonprobate property, then your will has no legal significance. It is not admitted to probate or filed with the court or any other public authority. This does not mean, however, that if you have only nonprobate property, you do not need a will. Property that is nonprobate now may become probate property prior to your death.

c. **SOME PROPERTY CAN BE EITHER PROBATE OR NONPROBATE**

Several types of property are not easily cataloged as either probate or nonprobate. These include life insurance and other contract property, businesses, and property that does not typically have documents of title, such as bearer bonds and certain tangible personal property.

1. Life insurance

If you own life insurance and name a beneficiary other than your estate, such as your spouse, and the beneficiary survives you, the proceeds will go to that person and will not be probate property. However, if you name your estate as the beneficiary, or if all your named beneficiaries die before you do, then the proceeds will be part of your estate and, therefore, probate property.

Some life insurance agents recommend that a husband own the policies on his wife's life and the wife own the policies on her husband's life. However, except in rare cases, cross ownership of life insurance policies accomplishes little. For example, Joan and Bob are married and each holds a policy on the other's life. If Joan dies first, Bob will have to deal through probate with the policy that Joan held on Bob's life. And if a couple holding policies on each others' lives decide to divorce, the cross ownership will complicate their financial matters.

2. Other contract property

Several kinds of contractual property normally do not become probate property because there is a named surviving beneficiary, but may become probate property because of the terms of the contract. Typical examples are —

(a) death benefits or annuities payable under retirement, pension, and profit-sharing plans and individual retirement accounts (IRAs),

(b) deferred compensation and other employer-provided death benefits,

(c) buy-sell arrangements for small businesses, and

(d) credit union share accounts with named beneficiaries.

3. Businesses

If you are in business for yourself, your interest in the business may be either as a sole proprietor, a partner in a partnership, a shareholder in a corporation, or a member in a limited liability company. Your ownership interest in each type of business may be probate or nonprobate property, depending on how you structure ownership.

(a) Sole proprietorship

A sole proprietorship is a business owned by one person. The assets of a sole proprietorship are probate property, and each asset (such as a vehicle, equipment, or inventory) is a separate asset of the probate estate.

(b) Partnership

A partnership is defined as "an association of two or more persons to carry on as co-owners a business for profit." A partnership is usually established by written agreement, but it can exist by a verbal agreement. There are two types of partnership: general and limited.

In a general partnership, all the partners are liable for partnership obligations and have a voice in partnership decisions. In a limited partnership, one or more partners, known as limited partners, are not liable for the partnership obligations, but are only liable to make any agreed-upon contribution to the partnership. A joint venture is a partnership, general or limited, for a specific, one-time business venture, such as developing and selling a parcel of real property.

A partner's interest is probate property unless the partnership agreement converts that interest into nonprobate property either by making the surviving spouse or some other person the successor in interest to the deceased partner or by making the partnership interest a form of joint and survivorship property.

(c) Corporation

A corporation is an artificial, separate, legal entity created by articles of incorporation. The shareholders own the business, and their ownership interest is reflected in stock certificates. Stock in a corporation may be held in either probate or nonprobate forms of property.

(d) Limited liability company

A limited liability company, or LLC, is a new, flexible form of business entity, authorized by Oregon law since 1993. It can be designed to combine the limited liability protection of a corporation with the income tax treatment of a partnership. A member's interest in an LLC can be held in either probate or nonprobate forms of property.

4. Property without documents of title

Normally, it is easy to tell whether property is probate or nonprobate because there is a deed, certificate, or other document of title, which indicates the form of ownership. However, some types of property do not have documents of title and may require special planning to minimize disputes over ownership when a person dies.

Two major types of such property are most tangible personal property (such as works of art and coin and stamp collections) and bearer bonds (which are bonds not registered in the name of the owner). A bearer bond may be redeemed by the person possessing it. Bearer bonds should be mentioned in your will and in any inventory of your property.

Tangible personal property can create problems in second marriages. Suppose each spouse brings certain furniture to a second marriage. They each intend that when the first spouse dies, the surviving spouse will have use of the furniture of the deceased spouse until his or her own death, at which time it is to go back to the children of the spouse that died first. One way to avoid a fight between the two sets of children after both spouses have died is to have a written agreement that identifies each spouse's separate property and states what is to happen upon the death of each spouse (see chapter 11).

Finally, there is a category of property over which you may have control while you are alive, but which you may not have power to dispose of at your death, because you do not own the property. This includes any property that you hold in a fiduciary capacity, such as trustee, guardian, conservator, or custodian, or that you hold as agent for someone else.

If you rent a safe deposit box in a bank in the names of two or more persons as joint tenants, it does not make the contents of the box joint property. The joint tenants could have an agreement making the contents joint property. This might make sense for contents without documents of title, such as a stamp or coin collection, or jewelry.

3
PROBATE PROPERTY

The most common examples of property subject to probate administration and also subject to disposition by your will are as follows.

a. SOLE OWNERSHIP

Any property that you own in your own name (and not jointly with any other person) and that has no type of limitation in terms of years or otherwise (such as a life estate) is your sole property and constitutes probate property.

For instance, if you own real property and the deed lists you as the sole grantee and does not put any limitations on the nature of the property interests granted to you, then you own that property in fee simple or fee title, and it passes as probate property.

This can apply to most other assets, including a bank account or stocks and bonds in your own name.

b. TENANCY IN COMMON

Tenancy in common is a form of joint ownership involving two or more persons, each owning an undivided interest in the property. Real property is frequently owned this way. For instance, a deed may read "to John Doe and Peter Smith, each an undivided one-half interest, as tenants in common."

Upon the death of a tenant in common, the deceased tenant's share passes according to his or her will, and is subject to probate administration. If there is no will, the share is subject to the laws of intestate succession. It does not pass to the surviving tenant in common.

The most obvious example of a tenancy in common is an express conveyance or deed of real property containing the required language. However, there are several situations involving property transactions that may create a tenancy in common without any express language.

1. Inheritances and devises

If property passes through probate administration and is distributable to more than one person, it is generally distributed to those persons as tenants in common. This may occur, for instance, when a brother and sister inherit real property from a parent and own it as tenants in common.

2. Personal property owned by spouses

If you are married, it may surprise you to learn that you may own some of your personal property with your spouse as tenants in common and not as joint tenants with any right of survivorship.

Under Oregon law, it is presumed that personal property is owned by spouses as tenants in common unless there is some express agreement providing for some other form of tenancy that clearly indicates survivorship. Express agreements of this kind can be made for any personal property, such as stocks and bonds or motor vehicles where there is a document of title. A stock certificate or motor vehicle certificate of title can, and usually does, expressly state that the property is owned jointly with right of survivorship.

However, because some personal property, such as furniture, furnishings, personal belongings, antiques, works of art, coin collections, and jewelry, does not have documents of title, if it were owned jointly by you and your spouse, it would be treated as owned as tenants in common.

If the wills of both you and your spouse provide that at the death of one spouse everything belongs to the other spouse, then there is no problem with this type of ownership. Nor is it a problem if there is total family harmony and your children assume and expect that your husband or wife will get all the jointly owned personal property when you die. But this is not always the case: if you die intestate leaving children from a previous marriage as well as a surviving spouse, your spouse would only get one-half of your share of the personal property and your children of the earlier marriage would be entitled to the other half.

The same problem can occur if you and your spouse lend someone money. Suppose the person to whom you loaned the money made a note payable to John and Jane Doe, husband and wife. The right to the proceeds from repayment of the loan would be considered a tenancy in common. When one of the spouses died, that spouse's one-half interest would pass as probate property.

A survivorship interest in the proceeds from the promissory note could be accomplished with either of the following two phrases: "John and Jane Doe, husband and wife, as joint tenants with right of survivorship" or "John and Jane Doe take the proceeds, not as tenants in common, but with right of survivorship, that is, upon the death of the spouse first to die, the surviving spouse shall be entitled to all proceeds."

3. Real property owned by divorced spouses

If a married couple owns real property as tenants by the entirety (see chapter 4) and continue to own the property jointly after divorce, either because the divorce decree does not deal with the property rights of each of the parties or because it directed that each shall have an interest in the property, the tenancy by the entirety is converted into a tenancy in common.

4. Invalid marriage

A man and woman who either think they are validly married or present themselves as validly married, but in fact are not, will be treated as owning any jointly owned property as tenants in common, even though a deed or contract of purchase may list them as husband and wife.

In one case, Fred and Rosemary were married and property was deeded to them as Fred and Rosemary, husband and wife. Normally this would create a tenancy by the entirety, meaning that when Fred died, the property would belong outright to Rosemary. Unfortunately for Rosemary, she and Fred were first cousins, and under Oregon law, marriages between first cousins are void. Fred died, and Fred's daughter, Fidelia, filed a lawsuit claiming that she was entitled to Fred's one-half interest as a tenant in common with Rosemary. The court agreed.

5. What you should know about a tenancy in common

There are a number of important points to consider about a tenancy in common.

- (a) Property may be owned in unequal shares. So, a deed creating a tenancy in common might read:

    To John Doe, an undivided one-third interest, and to Peter Smith, an undivided two-thirds interest, as tenants in common.

- (b) There may be more than two co-owners. There is no legal limit to the number, but there are practical limits to consider.

- (c) You can have a different form of ownership on top of the tenancy in common. For example, if two couples purchase a beach house together, each couple owns one-half interest as tenants in common. But each couple can also own their one-half interest as tenants by entirety with each other. The deed might read:

> To John Doe and Mary Doe, husband and wife, as tenants by the entirety of an undivided one-half interest, and Peter Smith and Betty Smith, husband and wife, as tenants by the entirety of an undivided one-half interest, as tenants in common.

If John dies first, Mary would come into sole title of their one-half interest. When Mary dies, her one half interest becomes probate property.

(d) Each share may be sold, mortgaged, given away, left in a will, or seized by creditors of the owner of the share without affecting the rights of the other co-owner and without his or her consent.

(e) Each co-owner is entitled to possession of the entire property, but not to the exclusion of the other co-owner. For example, when the Does purchased their one-half interest in the beach house, they did not buy just the left half. They own the whole house jointly with the Smiths.

(f) If one co-owner pays for necessary repairs, property taxes, insurance premiums, and liens and encumbrances on the property, he or she may claim reimbursement from the other co-owner. This is not true for the cost of improvements to the property that the other co-owner has not agreed to.

(g) If one co-owner receives rent or other income from the property he or she has to account to the other co-owner.

(h) If one co-owner reduces the value of the property without the consent of the other, he or she is liable for that share of the loss of value.

(i) If the co-owners cannot get along, the property can be partitioned by court action. If the property can be physically divided without reducing its value, the court will do so. Otherwise the court will direct the property to be sold and the proceeds to be divided between the co-owners.

(j) Co-owners can enter a written agreement amending and protecting their interests in the property. This is advisable especially for co-owners of rental or investment property. A tenancy in common agreement typically limits the right of one co-owner to transfer or encumber that co-owners's interest in the property without the consent of the other co-owner, and directs who will manage the property and how income and expenses will be handled.

c. REMAINDER INTEREST

It is possible for two persons to have successive interests in property. For instance, you could leave a piece of real property to two people: to one person for life, who then has what is known as a life tenancy with the right to use the property for his or her lifetime; and then to another person, whose interest begins upon the life tenant's death, and who has what is known as a remainder interest.

In this case, the person who has the remainder interest has a present legal interest in the property subject to probate administration, even though he or she does not have a present right to possess the property and may never possess the property if he or she dies before the life tenant.

If the person with the remainder interest, the remainderman, dies before the life tenant, then the heirs or the persons named in the remainderman's will are entitled to possession of the property when the life tenant dies.

Although this occurs most commonly with real property, it also can be used with personal property. A remainder interest can be given as a lifetime transfer through a deed or in a person's will. A provision in a will might state: "I give a life estate in X property to Jane Doe, and upon her death, I give the remainder to John Doe."

A typical lifetime deed may involve giving a remainder interest and reserving a life estate. It could read —

> John Doe, Grantor, conveys to Jane Doe all that real property situated in Multnomah County, Oregon, reserving unto Grantor a life estate for the term of the grantor's life.

d. INHERITANCE, DEVISE, OR TRUST DISTRIBUTION

If you are an heir of a relative who has died leaving probate property and no will, or if you are a devisee under that person's will, you have a legally recognized interest in that relative's property. If you die before you receive that property, your interest would be subject to probate administration.

Similarly, if you are the beneficiary of a revocable living trust, and the trustor has died, you have a legally recognized interest in the trustor's property. If you die after the trustor but before you receive distribution, your interest in the trust would be subject to probate administration.

e. OTHER PROBATE PROPERTY

There is a category of property in which the deceased may have no interest or title of record at the time of death, but which may nevertheless end up as probate property. This can happen, for example, if the deceased was incapacitated shortly prior to death and transferred all assets to another person, but the transfer is declared invalid because of the improper influence of the other person or because of the mental incapacity of the deceased. In that case, the personal representative of the estate can compel the other person to transfer those assets into the estate where they will be considered probate property.

Finally, assets that may not be probate property at the time you make out a will may end up probate property at the time of your death. An obvious example is property that you own jointly with right of survivorship with some other person, and that other person dies before you do. Or, you may own life insurance on your life designating certain beneficiaries, all of whom die before you do. In that event, the life insurance proceeds would become part of your estate and constitute probate property.

f. COMMUNITY PROPERTY

Property that would normally be considered probate property, but which you acquired with proceeds from the sale of property previously acquired as a married person in a community property state, may not be subject to probate administration in its entirety. Oregon is a common law state, which means that the rights of spouses to property are determined by the English common law tradition. The community property system, which has a different set of rules concerning the rights of spouses to marital assets, is derived from the Spanish tradition through Louisiana.

Oregon is surrounded by community property states (California, Idaho, Nevada, and Washington). There are also four other states that follow the community property tradition (Arizona, Louisiana, New Mexico, and Texas). It is not uncommon, therefore, for married couples who acquire property in community property states to move to Oregon.

Under Oregon law, any property you and your spouse acquired while married and living in a community property state retains its community property characteristics even if you sell the property in the community property state and purchase property in Oregon in your own name. If you were to die under those circumstances, one-half of your property would automatically belong to your surviving spouse even though the property is in your own name and would normally be subject to probate administration in its entirety. The other half would be subject to probate administration and disposition under your will. An express agreement between you and your spouse is needed if you want to change this situation.

Community property law will also determine how you own real property in a community property state, even if you are an Oregon resident. For instance, if you own a beach house in Washington jointly with your spouse, a half interest in the property will belong to your spouse when you die, and the other half will be probate property. If you want the entire interest to pass to your spouse by right of survivorship, as would happen in Oregon with tenancy by the entirety, you and your spouse must sign and record a community property agreement.

4
NONPROBATE PROPERTY

Nonprobate property does not pass under your will or under the laws of intestate succession. The most common type of nonprobate property is property owned jointly or concurrently by two or more persons with right of survivorship. That is, upon the death of the first co-owner, title automatically vests in the surviving co-owner.

Tenancies by the entirety, joint tenancies with right of survivorship in real property, and most joint tenancies with right of survivorship in personal property have similar attributes:

(a) Each co-owner is entitled to one-half of the rents and profits.

(b) Neither co-owner can force a severance of their joint interest in the property. That is, one cannot convert it into a tenancy in common by conveying the interest in the property to a third person. The one exception is joint tenancies in personal property created after 1974 where this right of severance does exist.

(c) Either co-owner can convey or encumber his or her own interest. However, all the grantee or creditor gets is an undivided interest subject to the right of survivorship in the other co-owner. This means if the other co-owner outlives the co-owner conveying the property, the grantee or creditor gets nothing.

These rules do not apply to joint bank accounts, which are discussed in section **g**.

a. TENANCY BY THE ENTIRETY

Tenancy by the entirety is a unique form of joint ownership of real property by husband and wife. Under a tenancy by the entirety, upon the death of the spouse first to die, the property belongs solely to the surviving spouse.

Contrary to the presumption of tenancy in common in personal property (see chapter 3), real property owned by spouses jointly is presumed to be owned as tenants by the entirety. Thus, a deed conveying property to John and Jane Doe, husband and wife, creates a tenancy by the entirety. This also applies to contracts to purchase real property in which the purchasers are husband and wife. A section in the contract stating that the purchasers are husband and wife is sufficient to create a tenancy by the entirety.

The one critical element of a tenancy by the entirety is that the parties are married to each other. If they are not married or if the marriage is invalid, they will own their real property as tenants in common.

b. OTHER SURVIVORSHIP — REAL PROPERTY

Persons other than spouses may own real property jointly with the right of survivorship. This form of ownership is not limited to two persons: it could be three or more persons, all owning interests in the property, with the property finally belonging to the last of the joint owners to die.

The language in deeds or contracts to purchase that establishes this ownership may be of two different types. It may read as follows:

> John Doe, Ronald Doe, and George Doe, not as tenants in common, but with right of survivorship, that is, the fee shall vest in the survivor of the grantees.

A second type of language would be as follows:

> John Doe, Robert Doe, and Ron Doe, as joint tenants with right of survivorship, and not as tenants in common.

c. SURVIVORSHIP — PERSONAL PROPERTY

It is also possible for husbands and wives or two or more persons, whether or not related, to hold personal property — tangible and intangible — jointly with right of survivorship. Generally, however, express language must be used to create such an interest. Thus, if two or more persons wish to own a car jointly with right of survivorship, that survivorship language must appear on the certificate of title issued by the Motor Vehicle Division. Similarly, if stocks or bonds are to be held jointly with right of survivorship, that language must expressly appear on the certificates.

There are two closely related forms of joint and survivorship ownership in Oregon with respect to personal property. One is known simply as joint tenancy and the other is generally called joint tenancy with right of survivorship. There is no difference between the two forms of joint ownership with respect to the survivor's right to sole ownership when the first joint owner dies.

The only significant difference between the two forms of ownership is that with a joint tenancy, one joint owner can sell or otherwise transfer his or her interest without the consent of the other joint owner. In property held jointly with right of survivorship, this is not possible.

d. SELLER-FINANCED REAL PROPERTY SALES

Seller-financed real property sales are an exception to the general rule that express language is needed to create a survivorship interest in jointly owned personal property. The seller's interest in a real estate contract or a note secured by a deed or mortgage is considered personal property because the seller's sole interest is the right to receive the balance of the purchase price. Seller-financed real property sales are in two forms: an installment real estate contract, in which the seller retains title as security until the purchase price is paid, or an immediate transfer of title in exchange for a promissory note for the purchase price secured by a mortgage or trust deed against the property.

Under Oregon law, where owners of real property sell real property and help finance the purchase, either by a real estate contract or by taking back a note secured by a trust deed or mortgage, and they own the real property either as tenants by the entirety or in some other form of survivorship ownership, if one joint owner dies before the purchase price is paid in full, the other joint owner is considered to have the right to receive payments of the deferred installments of the purchase price by right of survivorship. The estate of the deceased joint owner has no claim to the payments. No language of survivorship need appear in the contract, note, trust deed, or mortgage.

e. U.S. GOVERNMENT SECURITIES

Joint ownership of securities issued by the U.S. government is a second exception to the general rule requiring express language to create a survivorship interest in jointly-owned property. For instance, Series EE and HH Savings bonds can be owned in joint and survivorship ownership simply by listing the two owners' names with the word "or" between them. Savings bonds cannot be owned by joint owners as tenants in common.

Treasury Direct accounts, through which you can purchase Treasury bills, notes, and bonds, can be owned as tenants in common and in two forms of joint and survivorship ownership. One form, called "joint ownership with right of survivorship," requires registration in the names of two individuals, joined by the word "and" and ending with "right of survivorship." Transaction requests must be signed by both owners. This form of registration creates a conclusive right of survivorship.

The other form, called "co-ownership," requires registration in the names of two individuals, joined by the word "or." Transaction requests may be signed by either co-owner. This form of registration creates a conclusive right of survivorship, without any reference to survivorship.

f. LIFE ESTATES AND REMAINDERS

A life estate and remainder is a common planning tool in small estates where the home is the major asset. For example, it might be attractive to a widow who has a home and few other assets to leave everything to her adult son. In order to put her affairs in order and avoid probate, she could convey title to her house to her son and reserve a life estate for the remainder of her life. When she dies, the right to possess the property automatically goes to the remainderman, her son, without probate administration.

This gives her son an immediate legal interest in the house, or, in other words, he has part of the ownership of the house. However, the widow has exclusive right to the possession of the house for the rest of her life. When she dies, her son is entitled to possession. All he has to do to clear his mother's name off the title is to record a copy of the death certificate.

This sounds like good estate planning, but there are a number of disadvantages to life estates and remainders. Consider the following:

(a) The widow cannot sell or mortgage the house without her son's consent. If there were a falling out between the two and the son refused consent, the widow would be trapped with the house.

(b) If the son dies before his mother, the son's remainder interest becomes probate property and passes to his beneficiaries either by the terms of his will or by intestate succession. The widow may find that her house will become the property of someone she doesn't even know!

(c) If the widow changes her mind about her estate plan and wants to leave the house to someone else, she will have to persuade her son to deed the remainder interest back to her.

(d) If the son goes through a divorce, his remainder interest would be considered when assets are divided. It is unlikely, but not impossible, that the ex-wife could end up owning the remainder interest.

(e) The widow would not be entitled to the property tax deferral for persons age 62 or older.

(f) Life estate remainder relationships create a number of obligations between the widow and son. The widow, as tenant, is responsible for repairs to the property to ensure it does not decline in value. She is required to pay the interest and the remainder of the principal on any mortgages on the house. As well, she is required to pay fire insurance and property taxes on the home.

Life estates and remainders should be used with caution. If you want to give a son or daughter a remainder interest in your home while you are alive, make sure that you understand how much control of your home you are giving up. Even if there is a strong bond of mutual trust, you would be wise to prepare a written agreement outlining the rights and duties of the tenant and remainderman.

You can also provide in your will that at your death you will give a life estate in your home to one person and the remainder interest to another. Or, because of the rigid rules that govern life estates and remainders, you might want to put the home in trust, directing the trustee to permit the life tenant to live there for life and distribute the remainder at the life tenant's death.

g. JOINT BANK ACCOUNTS

In this section, joint account means a deposit account with a financial institution payable on request to one or more persons and includes a checking account, savings account, certificate of deposit, and share account. A financial institution includes commercial banks, savings and loan associations, and credit unions.

1. Features of joint accounts

Joint accounts are unique in two ways. First, the document establishing this particular type of joint ownership, the signature card, does not necessarily control who owns the funds in the account. It is prepared by the financial institution principally for its own protection.

If one joint owner withdraws funds from the account without the consent of the other joint owner, the other joint owner or the estate cannot hold the financial institution responsible. As a general rule, although the bank signature card is some evidence of the intent of the parties, it neither controls the rights of the joint owners while both are alive nor determines who owns the funds upon the death of the first joint owner. The courts must constantly struggle with the issue of what the intent of the parties was when the joint account was set up.

The second unique feature of joint bank accounts is that, generally, either joint owner can withdraw funds without the consent or knowledge of the other joint owner. Almost every other type of joint ownership requires the signature of all joint owners for any significant action relating to the asset.

Generally, people have two principal reasons for setting up a joint bank account:

(a) To ensure access to money for medical care and support in case of illness or incapacity

(b) To avoid probate

Unfortunately, many people set up joint bank accounts without considering the consequences. This lack of understanding has caused numerous problems in the past. Here are some examples.

Case #1: The joint owner who contributed to the fund may have to prove ownership if a judgment creditor of the other joint owner garnishees the account. This happened to a married couple, Corrine and Roy. Corrine had incurred a debt prior to her marriage to Roy. After they married, they set up a joint bank account with some of Roy's funds. Corrine's creditors got a judgment and they garnisheed the account. Roy proved that he had put in all the funds, so Corrine's creditors got nothing from the account. But Roy had to go through both a trial court and an appellate hearing before the case was resolved.

Case #2: Because of the unique ability of either joint owner to withdraw the funds from a joint bank account, temptation to abuse the trust placed in the non-depositor joint owner is great. In one case, John put money in a joint bank account with his son, Jim. Without John's consent, Jim took the money out and used it as a down payment on an apartment which he purchased in his and his wife's name. John got his money back from his son, but again he had to go to court.

Case #3: It is conceivable that a person could put funds in a joint bank account, say with a close relative, and end up having the funds not available as freely as they would have been if the joint bank account had not been set up. This is what happened to George. George, who was 87 years old at the time of trial, had set up a number of joint bank accounts with his daughter, Helen. According to Helen, she was to use the funds in the accounts for George's care, and any remaining upon his death would be her sole property. When George suffered a disabling stroke, a dispute arose between Helen and her brother Herbert and a step-brother, Arthur. After Herbert and Arthur were appointed guardians for George, Helen brought a lawsuit to determine the rights in the joint bank accounts. The court held that although it was clear that prior to his incapacity George, as the depositor of all the funds, could have closed the accounts without any liability to Helen, his conservators could not. The accounts had to be maintained in their joint ownership with right of survivorship and none of the funds could be used for any purpose except for necessary care, maintenance, and support for George.

2. Changes in law for joint accounts

Legislation was passed in 1978 that applies to joint accounts opened after January 1, 1978. It helps cure some, but not all, of the problems of joint accounts. The two major provisions of the legislation are the following:

(a) During the lives of the joint owners, the joint account belongs to them in proportion to the net contributions by each to the sums on deposit, unless there is clear and convincing evidence of a different intent. The statute also provides that a joint account may be paid on request to any one of the parties, and the financial institution is not required to ask about the source of funds received or about the proposed application of the withdrawn funds. However, this does not solve the problem of unauthorized withdrawals.

(b) Sums on deposit at the death of a party to a joint account belong to the surviving party unless there is clear and convincing evidence of a different intent at the time the account was created. This means that for joint accounts opened after January 1, 1978, it is more difficult for an estate of a deceased owner to establish a right to funds in a joint bank account.

In 1985, the U.S. Supreme Court decided that the Internal Revenue Service (IRS) can place an administrative levy on joint bank accounts if one of the joint owners owes the IRS back taxes. The administrative levy is a drastic collection procedure that enables the IRS to collect unpaid taxes without court intervention and without notice to the joint owner of the bank account who does not owe any taxes. If the joint owner who does not owe taxes owns all or part of the funds in the account, that owner will have to seek administrative review or file a lawsuit to recover the funds. Congress corrected this imbalance for IRS levies against bank accounts issued after June 30, 1989. Now a bank is not required to surrender funds on deposit in a bank account until 21 days after the levy. This gives the taxpayer a chance to notify the IRS of errors concerning the levy or ownership of the funds.

3. Avoiding joint account problems

There are several steps you can take to minimize the problems that can occur with joint accounts.

(a) If your sole purpose is to give a person funds in an account upon your death without probate, use a revocable trust account or a payable-on-death (POD) account. (See section **h.**) With this kind of account, you have sole control of the funds while you are alive, but upon your death, the funds belong to the beneficiary you designate without probate of your estate. This type of account is generally available only at savings and loan associations, not at commercial banks.

(b) If you want to give a person funds in an account at the time of your death and also have that person able to use those funds for your benefit if you become ill or incapacitated, but for no other purpose, you can use a joint account. However, you should also have a written agreement, signed by both you and the other joint owner, which states when and for what purposes the other joint owner may withdraw funds while you are alive, and also what he or she is to do with the funds when you die. Of course, if you keep the checkbook, passbook, or time certificate, this will give you some practical protection; such protection is not available with a statement account.

(c) If your sole purpose is to have someone pay your bills while you are ill or incapacitated, and you want the funds to pass under your will and be subject to probate, use an account in your own name, but give someone else a power of attorney to withdraw funds for your benefit. You should also have an agreement with that person concerning when and for what purposes the funds may be withdrawn.

(d) Whatever type of account you select, study the signature card and make certain you know what it says before you sign.

For further details on planning for incapacity, see chapter 13.

h. LIVING TRUSTS AND POD PROPERTY

The interest of a trustor under a living trust is nonprobate property. In the typical living trust, you, as trustor, will transfer title to all your probate property to a bank or individual as trustee with instructions contained in a written trust agreement requiring the trustee to deal with your property as you direct for the remainder of your life. When you die, the trustee who has title to your property will distribute your property according to the terms of the trust agreement and without probate. Living trusts are discussed in more detail in chapter 6.

Another type of living trust is the so-called "totten" trust or ITF (in trust for) deposit account, available at many financial institutions. This is a form of ownership of deposit accounts where you name yourself as trustee of the funds on deposit and have unrestricted use of the funds while you are alive, but at your death the financial institution distributes the proceeds to the beneficiary whom you have named on the signature card.

Payable-on-death (POD) deposit accounts are identical to totten trusts, but use different words to describe the parties. On POD accounts you are described as the owner rather than the trustee and have all rights of ownership while you are alive. When you die, the financial institution distributes the funds to the named payee or beneficiary.

United States savings bonds can also be owned on a POD basis. One significant difference from POD deposit accounts, however, is that you, as owner, may cash in a bond without the beneficiary's consent, but you cannot remove the beneficiary's name without consent.

Under the Uniform TOD ("transfer on death") Security Registration Act, which Oregon adopted in 1991, it is now possible to register stocks, bonds, and other securities with beneficiary designations, similar to POD deposit accounts.

If one person owned a security and wanted to name one beneficiary, the security would be registered: "John S. Brown TOD ("transfer on death") (or POD ("pay on death")) John S. Brown, Jr."

If two persons owned a security and wanted to designate a beneficiary after both had died, the security would be registered "John S. Brown and Mary B. Brown JT TEN ("joint tenants with right of survivorship") TOD John S. Brown, Jr."

It would also be possible to name contingent beneficiaries to take the security in the event the primary beneficiary failed to survive the owner.

The law applies to brokerage accounts as well as individual securities. However, the law does not require the registering entity to register securities in beneficiary form, and it permits the registering entity to establish the terms, conditions, and form of such registration. If you are interested in beneficiary registration for any of your securities, you must first check with your stock broker if it is your brokerage account or the issuing company or its transfer agent for individual securities to see if they permit such registration.

Because POD and TOD property goes to a named beneficiary at the owner's death, it does not go through probate. However, like life insurance and other contract property described in chapter 1, if all named beneficiaries predecease you, then this type of property can become probate property at your death.

5
INTRODUCTION TO TRUSTS

A trust is one of the most versatile and widely used estate planning tools. This chapter describes the general rules which apply to all trusts. The next chapter discusses the revocable living trust, one of the most popular trusts.

A trust is a three-way arrangement where one person transfers title to property to another person who holds and manages it for the benefit of a third person.

The property placed in the trust is known as the assets, the principal, the *corpus,* or the *trust res.* It is important to distinguish between the principal and income of the trust. The principal of the trust is the property of the trust as it may change in type through sale, purchase, and reinvestment. The income is the earnings from the principal, such as interest, dividends, and rent.

a. TRUSTOR, TRUSTEE, AND BENEFICIARY

The trustor is the person setting up the trust and whose property is placed in trust. This person is also called the settlor or grantor.

The trustee is the person who takes legal title to the trust property and manages it for the benefit of another person. The trustee may be an individual, a bank, a financial institution authorized by state law to engage in trust business, or, occasionally, a charitable organization. More than one trustee, or co-trustees, may act at the same time.

The beneficiary is the person for whom the trust is managed. There can be more than one beneficiary and may be classes of beneficiaries, such as children or grandchildren. There can be successive beneficiaries as well. For example, a child may receive benefits for all of his or her life after which one or more grandchildren start receiving benefits from the trust.

Some beneficiaries may be entitled to only the income of the trust. Others may be entitled to only the principal, and still others, to both.

b. CATEGORIES OF TRUSTS

There are two broad categories of trusts — living trusts (sometimes called *inter vivos* trusts), and testamentary trusts. You establish a living trust during your lifetime by a trust agreement which you and the trustee sign. You usually "fund" or transfer assets to the trustee during your lifetime.

There are two categories of living trusts, revocable and irrevocable. You can revoke or amend a revocable living trust, so long as you are alive and competent. The primary purposes of a revocable living trust are to avoid probate and plan for your incapacity. You cannot amend or revoke an irrevocable living trust. Irrevocable living trusts are used primarily for various tax purposes.

A testamentary trust comes into existence after you die and can be either in your will or in the post-death part of your revocable living trust. An example of a testamentary trust is a trust you establish to provide for the education of your children or grandchildren after you die.

c. ANATOMY OF A TRUST

The trust document will typically contain the following:

(a) A description of the property being placed in the trust

(b) Identification of the beneficiaries by name or by class and a description of the beneficiaries' rights under the trust

(c) The details on how long the trust will last. One of the advantages of a trust is that you can control how the property is managed and spent for one or more generations after your death. By law, however, a trust can continue only for the duration of the lives of the beneficiaries who are alive at the trustor's death, plus 21 years, or 90 years after the trustor's death, whichever is later.

(d) The name of the trustee. Alternative trustees can be named if the trustee fails to accept, dies, resigns, or is incapacitated.

(e) The distribution to the beneficiaries. For example, the trust may require regular distribution of income or it may require discretionary distribution based on a standard such as support, education, or medical needs.

(f) The powers of beneficiaries. It may give a beneficiary power to withdraw part of the principal out of the trust each year. This is in effect a power to order the trustee to distribute part of the principal to the beneficiary. A beneficiary may also have a power of appointment. For example, suppose you set up a trust naming your spouse as the income beneficiary and you want the principal to go to your children after your spouse's death. You can provide that the principal will go to your children but give your spouse a power of appointment to determine how much each child will get. This power normally would be exercised in your spouse's will. The beneficiary who is given the power of appointment is called the donee or the holder of the power. The person to whom the property is appointed by the donee is known as the appointee. The trust agreement will state who gets the property if the donee fails to exercise the power of appointment. Such a person is known as the taker in default.

(g) Directions to the trustee regarding investment of the trust assets. It usually gives the trustee discretionary power on how to invest, but it may list certain types of investments only, or it may direct the trustee to use certain investment counselors to determine how to make investments.

(h) Outline of trustee's powers. Generally a trustee is given all the powers necessary to carry out the terms of the trust. In Oregon, the Uniform Trustee's Powers Act applies to all trusts unless otherwise stated in the trust.

(i) Fee structure. The trust generally provides for a reasonable fee for the trustee. A financial institution charges an annual fee based on the value of the trust property.

d. REVOCABLE LIVING TRUST

A revocable living trust is set up during your lifetime. You may amend or revoke the trust, as long as you are alive and competent. A revocable living trust may become irrevocable if you become incompetent, and it necessarily becomes irrevocable when you die. A living trust is sometimes called an "inter vivos" trust.

A typical living trust has two parts. The first part sets out how the trustee administers the trust while the trustor is alive. The trustee may have charge of investments or make investments as the trustor directs. The trustee also makes distributions from the trust as the trustor directs. If the trustor becomes incapacitated, the trustee then takes charge of both investments and distributions.

The second part of a living trust deals with its administration after the trustor's death. This part is a substitute for the trustor's will and directs who is to get the trust assets. It may direct that after funeral expenses, debts, and death taxes are paid, the property be distributed and the trust terminated. Or it may direct that certain portions be kept in trust for particular beneficiaries for an additional period of time.

1. Funded revocable living trust

A trust is "funded" when property is transferred to the trustee and the trustee begins managing and distributing the trust property in accordance with the trust agreement. The funded revocable living trust is discussed in the next chapter.

Establishing a funded revocable living trust involves the following three steps:

(a) Preparing and signing a trust agreement

(b) Signing a "pour-over" will, which basically provides that if the trustor dies with any probate property, it will be transferred or "poured over" to the trust, so that the disposition of all the trustor's property will be made under the one document

(c) Transferring ownership of all of trustor's property to the trustee

A revocable living trust which is funded when it is signed has gained popularity recently as one of the best tools for planning your estate. The major benefits and drawbacks of the funded revocable living trust are explained in the next chapter.

2. The standby living trust

A trust may be "unfunded," which means that the trust agreement is signed, but the trustee has no property to manage until a certain specified event occurs, such as the death of the trustor, after which the trustee begins to manage the trust assets.

In a standby trust, the usual steps in creating a revocable living trust are taken. First, a trust agreement and pour-over will are signed, and the trustor signs and delivers to the trustee all documents required to transfer ownership of the property to the trustee.

However, the trustee does not record the deeds, send the stock powers to the stock transfer agents, or take any other steps to establish the trustee's ownership of the trust property. Instead, the trustee keeps the transfer documents and does nothing more in terms of managing trust property. Only when the trustor becomes incapacitated or the trustee receives instructions to begin active management does the trustee formally take title to the trust property. The assets are on "standby" ready to be managed, and the trust is unfunded until the triggering event, after which the trust is then considered funded.

The advantage of a standby trust is that you, as trustor, still appear to be the owner of all your property and can manage it yourself, but you have the benefits of a revocable living trust to provide for incapacity and avoid probate. If a bank is the trustee, it generally will charge only a nominal annual fee while the trust assets are held on standby.

The standby trust is rarely used, except when a bank is named as trustee, because of the uncertainty about whether financial institutions and title companies will recognize transfers of assets to the trustee if the trustee does not complete the transfers until after the death or incapacity of the trustor.

3. The self-declaration of trust

In a self-declaration of trust, you name yourself as trustee, thus making yourself all three parties to the trust agreement: trustor, trustee, and beneficiary. The same steps are taken as in setting up a funded revocable living trust with some other person as trustee. The most important requirement is the designation of a successor trustee, who will take your place as trustee in the event of your incapacity or death.

4. The revocable life insurance trust

The typical life insurance trust is an unfunded living trust, under which the trustor names a trustee, typically a bank, as beneficiary of life insurance policies on the trustor's life. The trustor pays the premiums and has all rights of ownership in the policy, including the right to borrow and to change beneficiaries. The trustee has no duties (other than safekeeping the policies) until the trustor's death, at which time the trustee obtains the proceeds from the policy and administers the proceeds according to the trust agreement. The principal benefit of the revocable life insurance trust is the ability to provide for distribution of the proceeds while avoiding the problems of probate.

e. IRREVOCABLE LIVING TRUSTS

An irrevocable living trust, like a revocable living trust, is set up during your lifetime, but may not be amended or revoked once it is set up. You give up the right to control property placed in an irrevocable trust.

Irrevocable living trusts are used primarily to minimize income, estate, and inheritance taxes. Because you must give up control of the property you transfer, you should use irrevocable trusts only with the assistance of tax experts and only if you are satisfied that the tax benefits that you expect to receive justify the loss of control of your property.

1. Irrevocable life insurance trusts

In an irrevocable life insurance trust, you either transfer cash to a trust, which purchases a life insurance policy on your life, or you transfer ownership of a policy on your life to a trustee and irrevocably relinquish all ownership. Such trusts are used as an estate and inheritance tax planning tool to exclude the proceeds from your estate for death tax purposes at your death.

2. Charitable remainder trusts

Suppose you want to make a substantial gift to your favorite charity while you are alive, but first want to make sure that your spouse receives the income from the gift for the rest of his or her life. You can do this by setting up an irrevocable living trust.

The only way to get an income, gift, and estate tax deduction for the value of the property that will go to the charity after your spouse's death is to use one of two forms of charitable remainder trusts. One is called an annuity trust and fixes the amount of your spouse's payments based on a percentage of the value of the assets initially transferred to the trust. The other is a unitrust and fixes the amount of your spouse's payments based on an annual valuation of the assets.

With an annuity trust the annual payments, once fixed, will not change for the remainder of your spouse's life. With a unitrust the payments will change each year, much like a variable annuity.

Charitable remainder trusts can also be set up as testamentary trusts in your will, where they would generate possible estate and inheritance tax savings, but no income tax savings.

f. TESTAMENTARY TRUSTS

A testamentary trust is set up under your will and does not go into effect or become funded until you die and the will is admitted to probate. In effect, the testator or testatrix is the trustor of a testamentary trust. This type of trust can also be included in the post-death or testamentary part of living trusts.

The possible uses of testamentary trusts are as varied as the needs of people making wills and the imaginations of the attorneys assisting them. Some of the more common reasons you may want to use testamentary trusts are —

(a) to provide for your children if you die while they are minors or until they are mature enough to handle their financial affairs.

(b) to provide for a physically or mentally handicapped spouse or child or other family member. These trusts can last for the rest of the person's life.

(c) to protect children of a previous marriage. A trust for this purpose could give your spouse the income and principal to maintain his or her standard of living, and the assets of the trust could be distributed to the children after your spouse's death.

(d) to minimize the risk that part of your estate would be dissipated by a spendthrift son- or daughter-in-law.

(e) to provide financing for college education for your grandchildren.

(f) to provide support for a dependent relative.

(g) to gain income, gift, inheritance, and estate tax savings.

g. TRUSTS AND TAX SAVINGS

Suppose you own all your property jointly with your spouse with right of survivorship, except for $200,000 of life insurance. Your property plus the life insurance is worth $700,000. If you die first, and you had named your spouse as beneficiary of your life insurance, there would be no federal estate tax to pay because of the unlimited marital deduction. If your spouse dies later with an estate of $700,000, there would be federal estate tax to pay.

However, if you had named a trustee as the beneficiary of your life insurance and left instructions to the trustee to make payments to your spouse for life and at your spouse's death distribute the remaining proceeds to your children, no tax would be paid at either your or your spouse's death. For a more detailed explanation of this trust, see chapter 17.

This is only one example of a possible tax savings. If you want detailed information, you should consult a tax expert.

h. THE DUTIES OF A TRUSTEE

The Oregon Supreme Court describes a trustee's duty as a "grave responsibility" involving a "fundamental duty of loyalty and good faith." The principal duties involved are as follows:

    (a) The duty to follow the terms of the trust agreement.

    (b) The duty to exercise good faith, diligence, and prudence in investing a trust property. This does not mean that the investments must always make a profit, but it does mean that the trustee should have the skills, or seek professional help, to invest wisely.

    (c) The duty to protect and preserve assets.

    (d) The duty to be loyal to the beneficiaries. A trustee cannot engage in any self-dealing, conflict of interest, act of fraud, or any other act of disloyalty.

    (e) The duty to account for all investments. This requires keeping accurate records of all receipts and disbursements of income and principal and prohibits the trustee from commingling trust assets with the trustee's own assets.

i. HOW TO SELECT A TRUSTEE

Because of the standards of conduct that a trustee must adhere to, the selection of a trustee itself is an important decision. This may not be difficult if you are setting up a revocable living trust for yourself, but it is still important to make a careful selection in case you become incapacitated or you are selecting a trustee for an irrevocable or testamentary trust that may last for many years.

Your choice might be a relative, friend, accountant, lawyer, or financial institution. See the Appendix for a list of names and addresses of financial institutions authorized to engage in trust business in Oregon.

1. Professional management

Banks are in the business of trust management and have both expertise and experience with investments and the complexities of trust administration, accounting, and taxation. An individual will probably not be able to offer you the same degree of expertise.

Whether you select an individual or a bank, you can place some control on your investments by requiring that certain trust property not be sold, designating the types of investments that are permissible, and requiring the trustee to use an outside investment counselor.

2. Impartiality

A trusted friend or relative may be more sensitive than a bank to the particular needs of your children or other beneficiaries. On the other hand, a bank will be impartial at all times. Suppose, for example, that you set up a trust for your son to last until he is 25 years old. Your son may resent the implication that he cannot handle his own affairs until he is 25. The trustee has to play the bad guy role while maintaining the terms of the trust. A bank will have no problem being impartial, and will not likely be tempted to favor one beneficiary over another.

3. Perpetual existence

It is unlikely that a bank will not be around for the duration of your trust. Unlike an individual, a bank will not become ill or incapacitated or die. A court will always appoint a successor trustee if an individual trustee dies, but then you might end up with someone as trustee you do not even know. You can minimize that risk by using a bank. If you want to name a friend or relative, it's a good idea to name one or more alternative trustees, name co-trustees, or give any adult beneficiaries the right to name a successor trustee.

4. Dishonesty

Unless a beneficiary files a lawsuit, a trustee is not accountable to the courts. This may tempt an individual to use trust assets for personal gain either through fraud or improper acts of self-dealing.

You could require the trustee to be bonded by a commercial surety company, but this adds to the cost of administering the trust and is seldom used. If you feel you need to require your trustee to be bonded, then you probably need to find a different trustee.

Although banks are not immune from fraud and conflicts of interest, such acts are rare. In addition, banks are governed by regulations that minimize the risk of loss to trust beneficiaries.

5. Trustee's fee

The fee may be the most practical consideration in choosing between a bank and an individual. It is generally 1% to 1.5% annually. Most banks have a minimum fee of $1,000 or more. This means that it usually is not worth it financially to use a bank as a trustee unless the trust property has a value of $200,000 to $250,000.

Many banks have fragmented fee schedules. For instance, for a living trust, many banks charge a one-time setup fee (typically $100 to $250), an annual fee based on a varying percentage (depending on the nature of the asset) of the value of the assets, a minimum annual fee (ranging from $1,000 to $2,500), additional transaction or hourly fees for specific services such as tax return preparation, and termination fees if you revoke the trust. Fees and fee practices vary widely among the banks, as do investment records, experiences, and expertise in specialized areas such as management of small businesses or farms.

An individual trustee is entitled to whatever compensation you provide for in the trust agreement. Often, family members who are acting as trustees will expect only modest compensation. However, an individual may have to hire professional advisers, such as an investment adviser or an attorney, resulting in costs to the trust that are normally included in a bank's annual fee. There may be adverse tax consequences from selecting a close family member as your trustee. Consult a tax advisor before you make your choice.

j. YOUR RIGHTS AS A BENEFICIARY

If you are a beneficiary of a trust and believe that your trustee is not doing a good job, and you cannot resolve the problem through negotiation, you can file a lawsuit to get a court hearing. By statute the court has the power to do the following:

(a) review the amount of compensation the trustee has paid itself and require the trustee to refund any excess amount,

(b) require the trustee to provide you with a report of all receipts and disbursements, an inventory of the trust property, and a summary of all transactions relating to the trust property, once a year, and

(c) instruct the trustee on the proper interpretation of the trust or on any matter relating to the administration, settlement, or distribution of the trust estate.

If the court finds that the trustee has been mishandling the trust it can —

(a) remove the trustee and appoint a successor,

(b) require the trustee to pay damages for any losses caused by breach of the trust, and

(c) deny or reduce the amount of the trustee's compensation.

6
THE FUNDED REVOCABLE LIVING TRUST

a. INTRODUCTION

As mentioned in the previous chapter, the living trust has gained popularity as a way of avoiding probate and as a vehicle for handling your affairs in case of incapacity. It has also been touted as a way of saving taxes.

When people talk about living trusts as a way of avoiding probate, they are referring to the funded revocable living trust, which will be called a "living trust" throughout this chapter.

Do not confuse a living trust with a living will. A living will is a popular name for a document you can sign directing that you do not want tube feeding or other forms of life support if you are terminally ill. In Oregon, a living will is called an advance directive (see chapter 13).

A living trust can be the centerpiece of your estate plan. However, it has no advantage over a will or other planning tools in saving taxes, and it is not for everyone. After reviewing living trusts, weigh the pros and cons (see section **h**.) before deciding whether it is right for you.

b. THE TRUST DOCUMENTS

Establishing a living trust involves two major steps: signing the trust agreement and related documents, and funding the trust by retitling assets into the name of the trustee. The basic documents are the trust agreement, a pour-over will (described in the last chapter), and one or more financial powers of attorney. In order to complete your estate plan, you should also consider signing such documents as an advance directive (see chapter 13), an anatomical gift card, and letters of instructions which may cover funeral and burial instructions.

A basic living trust agreement has two main parts. The first part directs how the trustee administers the trust during your lifetime. The trustee invests and manages the trust assets and makes distributions from the trust according to your directions so long as you are capable of giving directions. If you become incapacitated, the trustee then takes charge of both investments and distributions.

If you are able to handle your financial affairs yourself, then name yourself as the initial trustee and manage the trust. A successor trustee, named in the trust agreement, steps in and takes charge of your financial affairs if you suddenly become incapacitated, or if you ask the successor trustee to take charge.

If you are the acting trustee at your death, then your successor trustee steps in and settles your trust. If you need help with your financial affairs at the time you set up the trust, then you name someone other than yourself, such as a family member or bank, as the initial trustee who then will settle your trust at your death.

The second part of the basic living trust directs how your trust will be administered after your death. It contains the "dispositive provisions" (provisions that direct how your property will be distributed at your death) which would normally be in your will if you did not have a living trust. It may direct that after all your funeral bills, claims, expenses, and taxes are paid, your trustee is to distribute your trust estate to family members and then terminate the trust. Or it may direct that certain portions be kept in one or more testamentary trusts for particular beneficiaries for an additional period of time after your death.

Although one of the primary benefits of a living trust is probate avoidance, you still need a will, in case probate property gets overlooked or is intentionally kept in probate ownership and is not transferred to your trust during your lifetime.

There may be other reasons which may make it necessary to probate your estate; for instance, to make certain tax elections that only a personal representative can make, or to cut off creditors' claims. In the will, you name personal representatives, and you direct that if you die with any probate property, your personal representative is to transfer it or "pour" it over to the trustee of your living trust. This is the reason for the name, "pour-over" will.

The third major document you sign is one or more financial powers of attorney. Normally you name each trustee, including each successor trustee, as agent under the powers of attorney. The two primary purposes of this document are to enable an agent to transfer assets to your trust if you become incapacitated and to handle financial matters (such as filing your income tax returns) that cannot be handled by your trustee.

c. LIVING TRUSTS FOR MARRIED COUPLES

Married couples considering living trusts have several options. They can do a joint trust, or they can each have a separate trust. A trust is considered a joint trust if it has two trustors, regardless of the number of trustees.

1. The joint and survivorship living trust

The joint and survivorship trust is typically used by a married couple whose net worth is under $600,000 and is not likely to reach $600,000, and who own most of their property jointly with right of survivorship. Both spouses are typically the initial trustees. If one spouse dies or becomes incapacitated, the other spouse continues to act as sole trustee. After the incapacity or death of the first spouse, the other spouse has full legal control over the trust and may revoke or amend it.

2. The common joint living trust

This joint trust is used by married couples whose net worth exceeds $600,000 and who plan to minimize death taxes. It can also be used by couples who have children by prior marriages. It is basically two trusts in one, with each spouse's trust owning 100% of that spouse's separate property and 50% of all property owned jointly by the couple. The two trusts own the couple's joint property as tenants in common.

Upon the death of the first spouse, the joint trust is divided into two basic trusts. The first is a family trust, which consists of the deceased spouse's separate property and the deceased spouse's half interest in the joint property. The second is a survivor's trust, containing the remaining assets. The family trust may be divided into additional subtrusts for tax-planning purposes.

3. The community property joint living trust

This trust is designed for married couples who move to Oregon from a community property state. There are certain tax advantages to community property, which can be preserved by use of this trust, even though a couple moves to Oregon, which is not a community property state. This trust operates similarly to the common joint living trust, except that the joint property of the couple is owned by the trustees as community property rather than as tenants in common.

4. Separate trusts for each spouse

Each spouse can have a separate basic living trust. Married couples in second marriages and married couples who plan to do tax planning trusts, but prefer to separate their joint assets rather than have a common joint living trust, are the best candidates for separate trusts.

d. FUNDING THE TRUST

The second major step in establishing a living trust is to "fund" it by retitling your property into the name of the trustee. If your primary goal is to avoid probate at your death, all your property must be in your trust or in other forms of nonprobate ownership at your death. However, it may be inadvisable, impractical, or impossible to transfer all your property to your trust.

1. General funding rules

The following are some general funding rules:

(a) Each separate asset must be retitled. You cannot do a blanket transfer of all assets in a single document.

(b) Each asset must be listed in the name of the trustee rather than the trust. It is a peculiarity of trust law that a trust cannot own property. Title should be some version or abbreviation of this: "John Doe, or his successor in trust, as trustee of the John Doe Living Trust dated July 1, 199-"

(c) For some types of property, such as a life insurance policy or annuity, you list the trustee as beneficiary rather than owner.

(d) Oregon's small estate law permits transfer of probate property through the inexpensive use of a small estate affidavit if the value of the property is under certain thresholds (see chapter 16). You can thus keep some assets, such as a motor vehicle or a checking account, out of your trust.

(e) Certain tax-sensitive assets should not be transferred to a trust without the advice of a tax expert. Examples are tax-deferred annuities, individual retirement accounts (IRAs), stock in a closely-held corporation, incentive stock options, and rental real property with passive activity losses.

(f) When you retitle assets, financial institutions and title companies require information about your trust. Some financial institutions require you to complete a special form containing basic information about the trust, such as the date of the trust and the names of the acting and successor trustees. Others require you to provide them with a complete copy of your trust agreement.

One of the attractions of a living trust is that it can help you preserve the privacy of your financial affairs. In order to preserve your privacy, you should check to see if the financial institution will accept a certification of trust (see Sample #1), a form now sanctioned by Oregon law. A financial institution relying on the form is relieved from liability to any person. If a certification of trust is not acceptable, provide excerpts from your trust agreement, such as the first and last pages and the pages containing the trustees' powers. Try not to disclose the dispositive provisions of your trust, that is, the provisions that direct how your property will be distributed at your death.

(g) Once you have completed the funding of your trust, you should prepare a schedule, commonly known as Schedule A, listing all the assets in the trust. This will help you keep track of the assets in trust and will assist your successor trustee in identifying the assets which are in the trust. Preparing and signing the schedule to your trust does not excuse you from transferring assets to the trust.

2. Real property

You should transfer title to your family home, recreational home, and other real property to your trust by signing a deed and recording it in the county where the property is located. Generally you should use the same form of deed, typically a warranty deed, that was used when you acquired the property. The trustee should be listed as an additional insured party on your fire and liability insurance policies. The "insured" is the person who is protected by an insurance policy.

SAMPLE #1
CERTIFICATION OF TRUST

I, _John Smith_____, trustee of the _John Smith_____ Living Trust dated _May 3_____, 199_9_ make this certification pursuant to Oregon.

1. **Trust.** The trust is presently in existence. It was executed on _____May 3_____, 199_9_.

2. **Trustor and Trustee.** I am the trustor and am currently the sole trustee of the trust.

3. **Trust Powers.** Under the terms of the trust agreement, the trustee is given powers granted a trustee under the Uniform Trustee's Powers Act set forth in ORS 128.003 - 128.045, including the right to sell, exchange, assign, lease, encumber, or otherwise alienate all or any part of the trust estate on such terms as the trustee shall determine.

4. **Trustee's Mailing Address.** My mailing address as current acting trustee is: ___555 S.W. Zero Street___
_____Portland, Oregon   97200_____

5. **Trust Revocable.** The trust is revocable. Only the trustor can revoke the trust.

6. **Modification of Trust.** The trust can be modified, amended, or revoked by the trustor only.

7. **One Trustee Only.** I am acting alone as trustee and have authority to exercise trust powers alone.

8. **Taxpayer Identification Number.** The trust taxpayer identification number is _____.

9. **Title To Trust Property.** Trust property is to be titled as follows: __John Smith_____, or __his____ successor in trust, as trustee of the _John Smith Living____ Trust dated _May 3_____, 199_9_, as amended.

10. **No Change In Trust.** The trust has not been revoked, modified, or amended in any manner that would cause the representations contained in this certification to be incorrect.

DATED: _June 1_, 199_9_   _John Smith_____
                                            Trustee

STATE OF OREGON)
) ss.
County of Multnomah)

This instrument was acknowledged before me on _June 1_____, 19_99_, by ___John Smith_____ as acting trustee.

_____
NOTARY PUBLIC FOR OREGON
My Commission Expires:_____

If you have a loan secured by a mortgage or trust deed on the property, you should get the lender's consent. If you transfer rental property, you should also assign each lease or rental agreement to the trustee.

If you own a mortgage or trust deed, typically because you have loaned money or sold property, or if you have sold real property on contract, you can transfer your interest in these assets to your trustee. If you are receiving payments through a "collection escrow," then you may need to assign the collection agreement and deposit new deeds or similar documents in escrow. A collection escrow is a three-way contract between an escrow company and the buyer and seller. The buyer makes payments to the escrow company, who in turn sends the payments to the seller. The escrow company provides annual reports of all payments to both parties.

3. Other assets

If you own stocks and bonds from many different companies and hold all the certificates, you will simplify transfer of your securities to your trustee if you deposit all your securities in a brokerage account in the name of the trustee.

Transfer untitled property, such as your furniture, jewelry, and other tangible personal property, by a bill of sale or assignment.

e. TAX ASPECTS OF LIVING TRUSTS

In most aspects, living trusts are tax-neutral. A living trust will neither save you taxes nor cost you extra taxes.

1. Income taxes

During your lifetime, you are treated as owner of all assets in your trust for income tax purposes. Your trust is considered a "grantor" trust, which means that all income earned on trust assets is deemed earned by you.

If you are your own trustee, then when you transfer assets to your trust, you continue to use your own Social Security number as your taxpayer identification number. You do not need to file a separate income tax return for the trust.

If you are not your own trustee, then the trustee must obtain a separate taxpayer identification number and file annual informational income tax returns. However, your trust is still considered a grantor trust and all trust income is taxed to you and not to the trust.

At your death, your trust becomes an irrevocable trust and ceases to be a grantor trust. Your trustee must file annual trust income tax returns and your trust must pay tax on any income that is not distributed to your beneficiaries during the year the trust receives the income. These returns are similar to the income tax returns which a personal representative would have to file if your estate required probate.

2. Gift taxes

Because you have a right to revoke your trust, you do not make a gift for federal gift tax purposes when you transfer assets to the trust. However, if you are married, you must exercise care in transferring assets to your trust or trusts. For instance, there may be a gift for gift tax purposes if an asset owned by one spouse is transferred to a common joint living trust or to a separate trust established by the other spouse.

If you plan to make gifts of property out of your trust, for example, to your children under the $10,000 gift tax annual exclusion, then you should plan to follow a two-step procedure. You should first withdraw the asset from your trust, then make the gift.

For instance, if you want to make a gift of $5,000 to a child, you should first withdraw this amount from the trust and put it in a bank account in your own name, then write a check out of that account to the child. If you do not, and if you were to die within three years after the date of the gift, then you will lose the benefit of the annual exclusion.

3. **Death taxes**

Placing assets in a living trust does not save you any federal estate or Oregon inheritance taxes. Because of your right to revoke your trust up to the moment of your death, all assets in your trust at your death are considered part of your gross estate subject to death taxation.

Many promoters of living trusts tout the death tax savings which you can obtain from a living trust. Typically they are talking about the so-called bypass or credit shelter trusts used by married couples and described in chapter 17. Such trusts can be set up in either a will or a living trust, and setting them up in a living trust is neither better nor worse than setting them up in your will.

f. PERIODIC REVIEW

If you establish a living trust, then periodic review, perhaps once a year, is essential to assure that you achieve the benefits of the living trust. The purpose of the review is to assure that your living trust reflects your current wishes and goals and that all or substantially all your assets are in your trust or in other nonprobate forms of ownership. You should review your trust agreement and related documents as well as the title documents to all your assets.

Periodic review is more essential with a living trust than with a will. If you purchase or inherit assets after you establish a living trust, then make sure that your new assets are in your trustee's name and not in your name individually. If you leave new assets in your individual name, then they will be probate assets at your death, requiring a probate of your estate.

You should review, and if necessary, revise your trust agreement because of changes in your circumstances. One example is your marriage, remarriage, divorce, or annulment. Your marriage or remarriage automatically revokes your will, and the dissolution or annulment of your marriage automatically revokes any provision in your will for your former spouse. This is not true, however, with a living trust. A marriage or divorce does not automatically revoke or amend your living trust unless you so provide in your living trust.

g. SETTLEMENT AT TRUSTOR'S DEATH

A primary benefit of a living trust is the avoidance of probate at your death. Having a living trust, fully funded, to avoid a probate at your death, does not necessarily mean that there will be no delay or costs in settling your affairs.

Your trustee must follow many of the same steps that a personal representative must follow if your estate required probate. The primary differences are that your trustee can settle your trust without court supervision, without filing an inventory or accountings with the court, without the formal notices to creditors and to heirs, and without regard to the various probate waiting periods and deadlines.

Your trustee's primary duties are: to collect, take control of, and manage all assets, and preserve and protect assets; to pay all debts and claims against the trust; to pay all income, gift, and death taxes; and to distribute the assets in accordance with the trust agreement.

These steps cannot be accomplished within a day, a week, or even a month. A simple trust can probably be settled within 60 to 90 days after the trustor's death. A typical settlement period is three to six months. If your estate is large enough to require the filing of death tax returns, settlement may take a year or longer.

There will also be costs incurred in settling your trust. Your trustee will probably need the assistance of an attorney, but attorney fees should be lower than if your estate required a probate. Your trustee may also need a tax advisor, one or more appraisers, and other professional advisors.

h. THE PROS AND CONS

This section outlines some of the major benefits and drawbacks of the revocable living trust. The advantages include the following:

(a) A living trust is an effective tool for handling your financial affairs if you are incapacitated. In the trust agreement, you can direct who will handle your affairs by naming a co-trustee or successor trustee. You can also state how incapacity will be determined and how your affairs will be handled.

Generally, a trust is more dependable than a power of attorney, which may not be accepted by banks, insurance companies, stock brokers, or title companies. A trust is also generally preferable to a court-supervised conservatorship, which is expensive and cumbersome and makes the facts of your incapacity and the nature and extent of your financial affairs matters of public record.

(b) A living trust can avoid the delay and expense of probate. A trust will survive you, and on your death there is no need to probate property in your trust because the legal ownership of assets in the trust is with the trustee.

Probate is a court proceeding open to the public. A living trust is a private arrangement and your financial affairs are not subject to public scrutiny at your death. If you have real property in more than one state, a living trust will save you the expense of multiple probates.

(c) A living trust is a flexible estate planning tool. You can create a self-administered living trust where you name yourself as trustee and beneficiary. With this type of trust, you continue to manage and direct your investment portfolio as you do now. You have full discretion over how to invest your assets and how to use the income from those assets. You have the additional protection of naming a successor trustee to take over the management of your trust if you die or become incapacitated. If you prefer to have help with your investments, you can select and name a professional manager, such as a bank or investment advisor, as your trustee.

(d) A living trust can help assure a coordinated disposition of all your property. When you rely primarily on a will, it is easy to forget that many of your assets, such as life insurance and retirement benefits, may not go through probate and to overlook the need to coordinate the disposition of your probate and non-probate property.

Some of the disadvantages include the following:

(a) A living trust is more expensive and time consuming to set up than a will, and is a more complicated document than a will. Attorney fees for a living trust will be higher than for a will. You may have recording and other transfer fees. If you use a bank as trustee, you will have annual trustee's fees to pay.

(b) In addition to preparing and executing the trust agreement, you must also transfer ownership of all assets into the name of the trustee. This forces you to organize, review, and redo title documents and beneficiary designations to all the property you wish to put into trust. It has been likened to probating your own estate while you are still alive.

(c) Once the trust is in place, you must regularly monitor your affairs to assure that all your property is in the name of the trustee. In addition, if you are acting as your own trustee, you may find it more difficult to deal with stock transfer agents, life insurance companies, and title insurance companies.

(d) Unlike a probate, with a living trust the time frame within which creditors' claims may be filed is not shortened so as to bar claims after your death.

(e) During probate, a court supervises your personal representative. If he or she misbehaves, your beneficiaries can voice their objections. The personal representative must file accountings with the court, and probate records are subject to public scrutiny, which encourages honest, punctual, and responsible administration of probate estates.

There are no such built-in incentives for a trustee settling a living trust at your death. The trustee proceeds to settle your trust (or fail to settle it) without court supervision or public scrutiny; beneficiaries only know whatever the trustee tells them. If a trustee mismanages your trust after your death, a beneficiary must file a lawsuit against the trustee to try to correct the trustee's misdeeds. There are few areas of trusts where you have to trust your trustee more, in the literal meaning of the word, than in your selection of the trustee of your living trust.

(f) There are no significant tax benefits or drawbacks with a revocable living trust. For income, gift, and estate tax purposes, you are still treated as the owner of all the property in your trust. Contrary to what some trust promoters claim, a living trust is no better or worse than a will as a planning tool for minimizing or eliminating death taxes.

In summary, you are probably a good candidate for a living trust if you are at or beyond retirement age and are more concerned about preserving and managing your estate than building it, or if you have become concerned about your own capacity to manage your financial affairs.

7

WHAT HAPPENS WHEN YOU DIE WITHOUT A WILL?

a. INTRODUCTION

This chapter might well be subtitled "The Costs of Neglect" because of the frequently unexpected consequences and the unnecessary costs that can result when someone dies with probate property and without a will.

One of the risks is the possibility of distribution of your probate property to your "laughing heirs," that is, distant relatives you never met or knew. Another risk is the possibility of extra costs in settling your estate. These extra costs are built into a probate system in part to protect your heirs from your own lack of planning.

This chapter deals only with what happens to your probate property when you die without a will. Your nonprobate property will not go to your heirs; it will go to those persons who are the designated recipients based on the form of nonprobate property. For example, suppose you die without a will. You leave a house, a savings account in your own name, some life insurance with a named beneficiary, and some securities owned jointly with right of survivorship with another person. Your house and savings account will go through probate to your heirs, but your life insurance proceeds and securities will not. They will go to the named beneficiary and the other joint owner.

b. WHO ARE YOUR HEIRS?

If you die without a will, your heirs are determined by Oregon's laws of intestate succession, which are sometimes called the laws of descent and distribution. The purpose of these laws is to approximate the desires of the person who dies intestate, that is, the person who dies with probate property and without a will. However, no law can anticipate every individual's specific desires. If you want all your wishes to be met, you should have a will.

To be your heir under the laws of intestate succession, a person must either be your spouse or must be related to you by blood or adoption. This means that none of your probate property will go to close friends, a favorite charity, or to relatives by marriage like a son-in-law or step-children. This is one of the costs of neglect.

1. Heirs and devisees

The term "heir" refers solely to a relative who is entitled under law to a share of your probate property when you die without a will. This term should not be confused with the word "devisee," which refers to any person or organization that is entitled to a share of your probate property under the terms of your will.

2. Surviving spouse

To be considered legally married, a couple residing in Oregon must have their marriage solemnized. Oregon requires a ceremonial marriage and does not recognize common-law marriage, unless it was consummated in a state that recognizes common-law marriages (see chapter 11). However, for the limited purpose of inheritance under the intestate succession law, Oregon recognizes a person as a surviving spouse, even though the person was not married to the decedent, if the person meets certain requirements. This change in the law was first enacted in 1993 and amended in 1995.

A person qualifies as a surviving spouse for inheritance purposes (even if the person was not married to the decedent at the decedent's death) if he or she meets the following requirements:

(a) The person and the decedent cohabited for a period of at least ten years prior to the decedent's death.

(b) The ten-year period ended not earlier than two years before the decedent's death. This provision is intended to cover the possibility that the couple did not cohabit for a short period of time because one or both were in a nursing home.

(c) The couple was not married to each other and then divorced. A divorced spouse of the decedent cannot qualify.

(d) During the ten-year period, each person was capable of entering a valid marriage contract. To be capable of entering a marriage contract in Oregon, each person must be at least 17 years of age, must be physically and mentally capable of marriage, and must not be first cousins or any nearer kin to each other.

(e) During the ten-year period, the couple mutually assumed marital rights, duties, and obligations.

(f) During the ten-year period, the couple held themselves out as husband and wife, and acquired a uniform and general reputation as husband and wife.

(g) During at least the last two years of the ten-year period, the couple was domiciled in Oregon.

(h) Neither the person nor the decedent was legally married to another person at the time of decedent's death.

This definition of surviving spouse applies only for inheritance purposes. If the decedent left a will, then the will controls how much, if any, property the person receives. If the will omits the person, the person cannot elect against the will as a surviving spouse nor exercise any other rights that a surviving spouse has against a decedent's estate. If the decedent left no will, then the person is entitled to a share of the estate as a surviving spouse, to live in the family home, and to support during probate administration (see chapter 11 on marriage).

A person who qualifies as a surviving spouse under this law is eligible to receive social security survivor's benefits.

3. Issue and lineal descendants

A lineal descendant is any living child, grandchild, great-grandchild, or any later generation in the same line of descent. The term "issue" has more limited meaning. It refers to any living lineal descendant except a lineal descendant of another living lineal descendant.

Only lineal descendants who are issue can inherit from you. For example, suppose you had two children, Bob and Ron. Bob has one child, Aaron, and Ron has one child, Susan. Bob dies before you do so at your death you have three lineal descendants: Ron, Aaron, and Susan. But only Ron and Aaron are your issue. Susan is not because she is the lineal descendant of a living lineal descendant, that is, Ron's daughter. Susan would not inherit from you.

4. Representation

Representation refers to the method of determining what each heir is entitled to when they are of unequal kinship. Suppose that you die without a surviving spouse and are survived by your daughter, Mary, and by the two children of a deceased daughter, Ruth. Mary would receive 50% of your probate property. Ruth's two children would split her 50% share, each receiving 25% of your probate property. Ruth's two children receive their share "by representation."

If your heirs are of equal kinship, they share your probate property equally. If, in the example above, both your daughters died before you, all your grandchildren would share equally in your probate property.

c. WHO GETS WHAT?

If you die without a will and with probate property, your heirs and their share of probate property is determined as follows:

(a) If you die survived by your spouse but no children or other issue, or if all your children or other issue are also issue of your spouse, your spouse gets all your probate property.

(b) If you are survived by a spouse and children or other issue, and if one or more of your issue are not issue of your spouse (as might occur in a second marriage), your spouse gets 50% of your probate property and your issue share the remaining 50%.

(c) If you are survived by children or other issue, but no spouse, your issue share all the property.

(d) If you die without a surviving spouse or issue, then your parents are your heirs. If both parents are alive and married to each other at the time of your death, they will take your real property as tenants by the entirety and your personal property as joint tenants with right of survivorship. If they are not married to each other they would take all your property as tenants in common. If you are survived by only one parent, that parent gets all your probate property.

(e) If you die without any spouse, issue, or parents, any brothers or sisters will be your heirs. Your brothers' and sisters' issue (i.e., your nephews and nieces) are covered by the rules of representation.

(f) If you have no heirs in the above categories, then your grandparents are next in line. If all four grandparents are alive, each of them would get 25% of your probate property. The same rules of representation apply to your grandparents' issue, so that uncles and aunts and their children (your cousins) become your heirs if any of your grandparents die before you.

(g) If you have no relatives in the above categories, the state of Oregon becomes your sole heir. This is known as "escheat." All your probate property will be distributed to the Division of State Lands.

If you own probate real property in more than one state, and you die without a will, your estate settlement will be more complicated. Your heirs of probate property will be determined by the laws of intestate succession of the state where the real property is located. Although most state laws are similar to Oregon's, they are not exactly the same. A will would avoid any confusion.

d. SPECIAL RULES GOVERNING HEIRS

1. Afterborn heirs

An heir conceived before your death and born after your death inherits as though he or she were alive at your death.

2. Survivorship by 120 hours

If an heir dies within 120 hours after you die, he or she is considered to have predeceased you. This may make the probate of the heir's estate unnecessary, where that heir dies a short time after the deceased.

3. Persons of the half blood

Persons of half blood inherit the same share they would inherit if they were of full blood. For instance, if you had been married twice and have a daughter by each marriage, your daughters are half-sisters to each other. However, both would be considered your heirs and heirs of each other.

4. Adopted children

Generally, under Oregon law, an adopted person is treated as a natural child of the adoptive parents for all purposes of intestate succession, and ceases to be treated as a child of the natural parents. This means that if you are adopted, your issue are all treated as if you were the natural child of your adoptive parents. Similarly, your adoptive parents and their issue or other heirs are treated as if your adopted parents were your natural parents.

For example, suppose an adopted child were to die without spouse or issue after his or her adoptive parents had died, and suppose further that the adoptive parents had natural children of their own. The natural children would be entitled to inherit from the adopted child as if that child had been a natural brother or sister.

The two exceptions to the general rule that an adopted person ceases to be the child of both natural parents are:

(a) If you have a child and you then marry or remarry, and the child is adopted by your new spouse, the other natural parent of your child would no longer be considered the parent, although you would.

Take the situation of a divorce where the mother is granted custody of a minor child and the father loses all interest in the child. The mother remarries and the new husband wants to adopt the minor child to seal the new family relationship. The natural father, desiring to be relieved of his child support obligation, willingly consents, and the parent-child relationship between the natural father and the child is terminated. If the natural father later dies without a will, the minor child would not inherit from him, but the child would inherit from the natural mother if she died without a will.

(b) If a natural parent dies, the other natural parent remarries, and the child is adopted by the new spouse, the adopted child continues to be considered a child of the deceased natural parent; in effect, the child is considered as having three parents for purposes of intestate succession.

For example, say a father dies, the mother remarries, and the new husband adopts the child. Then the natural father's mother, who would be the child's grandmother, dies without a will. The child would be considered an issue of his grandmother for purposes of intestate succession and would take all or part of the natural father's share of the grandmother's estate by representation.

5. Unmarried parents

In Oregon, a child born out of wedlock has the same rights of inheritance as any natural child. The only requirement is that the father's paternity of the child born out of wedlock must be established during the child's life, either by appropriate legal procedures, or by the father's written acknowledgment.

e. OTHER COSTS OF NEGLECT

Besides not being able to choose your own heirs, you will create other problems if you die without a will. For example, the probate court will select the personal representative for your estate. When there is no will, this person is known as the administrator (or administratrix, if female). The court gives preference in the following order for the appointment:

(a) Your surviving spouse, or a person selected by your spouse

(b) Your nearest relative or a person selected by your nearest relative

(c) Certain government officials

(d) Any other person

The personal representative must file a surety bond to protect the heirs and creditors from any breach of duty. A commercial surety bond will cost about $5 per $1,000 of value of probate property, and must be renewed annually. In a will, the testator typically waives the bond requirement to save this expense.

If an heir is a minor, the court will require that a conservatorship be established to protect the inheritance unless it is small enough to distribute to some responsible adult or financial institution. If a conservatorship is required, you will not have any say who will be appointed. A surviving parent is not permitted to use the minor's inheritance to support the child.

If you leave a minor child and the other parent is deceased, the court must appoint a guardian. If you have no will, the court might consider a relative that you would think totally unfit to care for your child.

You also reduce the risk of arguments among heirs by having a will. Suppose, for example, that you had three parcels of probate real property and three heirs entitled to equal shares. The heirs could agree to take one parcel each, but if they cannot agree, the personal representative would have to sell the three parcels and split the proceeds. If you have a will, you can direct who gets what property and thus minimize the risk of valuable family property being sold.

8
ALL ABOUT WILLS

This chapter focuses on the mechanics of making a will. Who can make a will? What are the requirements of a valid will? How is a will revoked?

a. WHAT THE WORDS MEAN

There are several important terms necessary to an understanding of a discussion of wills.

(a) The person making the will is called a *testator* if male, a *testatrix* if female.

(b) A *personal representative* is the person or financial institution you name in your will to settle your probate estate. This person is also called an *executor* (*executrix* if female).

(c) A *codicil* is an amendment to a will. A codicil must meet the same requirements for validity as the will.

(d) *Devise* (verb) means to give or dispose of property under a will. A *devise* (noun) is a gift or disposition of property under a will.

(e) A *devisee* is a person entitled to receive property under a will. This person may also be called a beneficiary, recipient, or distributee.

Today, Oregon law makes no distinction between gifts of real and personal property under a will.

b. WHAT IS A WILL?

A will is a document in which you direct who will receive your probate property at death and who will be in charge of settling your estate.

A will is unique among legal documents because it has no legal effect until you die. This unique feature of wills has several aspects:

(a) You can amend or revoke your will any time prior to your death, provided you have the mental capacity to do so. Even if you have made a contract not to change your will, that contract will not bar you from changing or revoking your will, but it may subject you or your estate to a lawsuit for breach of contract.

(b) A will does not affect your right and control of your probate property. You continue to be free to buy, sell, give away, consume, mortgage, or otherwise deal with your property without restriction. Even if you leave a specific item of property to a specific person you are not restricted from selling the item or even giving it to someone else while you are alive.

(c) Conversely, no person to whom you leave property in your will has any legal claim to the property until you die. As long as you are alive, your devisees only have an expectancy, which may or may not ripen into a legal claim. You may change your will, outlive the devisee, or sell or give away the property. This is why it may be imprudent to tell people that you are leaving property to them. A will determines the distribution of probate property that you own at death. Therefore, a will must take into account the possible events that may occur between the date you make the will and the date of your death.

c. WHAT MAKES A WILL VALID?

To make a valid will, you must meet these four requirements:

(a) You must be over the age of majority.

(b) You must have the mental capacity to make a will.

(c) The will must be the product of your own mind and not of someone else's, whether because of improper or undue influence, duress, or fraud.

(d) You must follow the required formalities.

You must meet the same requirements to make a valid amendment or codicil to your will.

1. Age requirement

To make a valid will, you must be 18 years of age or older or be lawfully married. A 17-year-old can marry. Thus, a 17-year-old married person can make a will.

2. Mental capacity

The second requirement is that you be of sound mind or that you have what is known as "testamentary capacity." To have testamentary capacity you must meet the following conditions:

(a) You must understand the nature of the act in which you are engaged (i.e., you understand that you are signing a document declaring the manner in which you want to dispose of your property at your death).

(b) You must know the nature and extent of your property. You do not need to know the exact size of your estate, but you must have a genuine knowledge as to its nature and extent.

(c) You must know, without prompting, who your heirs are (i.e., those persons who would be entitled to inherit from you if you did not have a will). This is discussed in chapter 7. Your heirs are also known as your "next-of-kin" or the "natural objects of your bounty."

(d) You must make rational disposition of your property.

You must have testamentary capacity at the moment you sign your will. Whether or not you have such capacity before or afterwards is not controlling. You do not need the same level of mental capacity to make a will as you do to convey property or enter contracts. Thus, you can have testamentary capacity even though you are mentally retarded, have mental or severe physical illness, are on your death bed, are under a guardianship or conservatorship, make an eccentric disposition of your property or have eccentric living habits, or are deaf, dumb, blind, illiterate, or speak a foreign language. In each case, it depends on whether or not you meet the four requirements at the moment you make your will.

Here are some examples from Oregon court decisions where persons were found to have testamentary capacity in spite of serious mental or physical problems.

(a) Mental retardation

In his childhood, Alvin had an illness diagnosed as "brain fever," which retarded his mental development. He spent nine years in the first grade and never learned to read and write, but his mother did teach him to sign his name. He was slow in conversation and slow to understand. Nevertheless, he was generally self-sufficient and knew all about his property and how to protect his interest in it. When he made a will leaving everything to his friends and excluding his heirs, the court found that he did have testamentary capacity and upheld the will.

(b) Mental illness

Aletha was found to have testamentary capacity even though she had been mentally ill both before and after she signed her will. After she signed her will in her attorney's office, she was taken into custody by the police and confined until she was committed to the state hospital the next day. Her illness on occasion took the form of auditory hallucinations, such as hearing voices, and she had a persecution complex which was described as a schizophrenic reaction.

In another example, Joan was 84 years old when she signed her will. She had chronic bronchitis, arteriosclerosis, influenza, a bad cough, and was delirious and weak. She heard voices, believed in the presence of a man in her house who was not there, and she frequently heard cats on her roof, although none was there. She also was found to have testamentary capacity.

(c) Extreme physical illness

Randi signed her will when she was 85 years old, the day after she suffered an acute congestive heart failure. Four days later she died. James signed his will the day before he died. Both wills were found valid.

(d) Eccentric living, behavior, and disposition

Frank was described as an oddball. He became increasingly slovenly shortly before his death and his eating habits and person were incredibly filthy. He failed to care for and often did not feed his livestock, and dead animals rotted about his farm. He took care of nothing and lived on four dozen eggs a week, which he cooked in a pressure cooker. He slept in his clothes and wore rain gear and rubber boots continuously. In his will he ignored his sister and gave $1 to a brother who died a month before the will was signed. In spite of all this, the court held that Frank had testamentary capacity.

3. Undue influence

The next requirement for a valid will is that it be the product of your own mind and not of someone else's. A will resulting from fraud, duress, or the strong influence of some other person is considered the product of someone else's mind.

For instance, a will can be the result of fraudulent conduct by a beneficiary, either dealing with the signing of the will directly, such as misrepresenting its contents, or misrepresenting the facts on which the will is based.

For example, Alise was in her eighties in 1947, weighed about 285 pounds, was strongwilled, had a good mind, and expected absolute honesty from those dealing with her, believing, according to the court, the old adage that a man's word is his bond. When a promise was made to her, she expected and demanded that it be kept as given. She was particularly fond of one of her cousins, Margot, who lived in Illinois. Alise had an agreement with Margot that should Alise ever become seriously ill, Margot would come to her. Alise became ill in July, and Margot came out and stayed with her until August 14, when Alise signed a will leaving the bulk of her estate to her cousins, including Margot.

In September, Alise became seriously ill again and went to bed and never got up. At this point, Clara, who was the wife of Alise's stepson, entered the picture. Alise directed Clara to write Margot and have her come out because of Alise's illness. Clara, however, did not write, although Margot regularly wrote to Alise. Because of Clara's refusal to communicate with Margot, Alise developed a growing distrust and loss of confidence in Margot because she did not keep her promise to come when Alise got sick. As a result, in December, 1947, Alise changed her will, leaving only $1,000 to Margot and her cousin, and the residue of her estate to Clara and others. The court concluded that Alise was the victim of Clara's deception, that it was Clara's failure to inform Margot that she should come and her failure to communicate Margot's letters to Alise that caused Alise to substantially disinherit Margot. The December, 1947, will was declared invalid as a result of Clara's conduct.

A will is also invalid if a person influencing the will by his or her conduct gets an unfair advantage by devices which reasonable people would consider improper. This does not prevent advice-giving or kindnesses or confidential relationships between you and a beneficiary. However, if a beneficiary under a will obtains his or her share by means of an unfair advantage, subterfuge, misrepresentation, or other conduct, the will will be set aside.

For instance, in 1971, Sophia signed a will naming one of her two daughters as her sole beneficiary. Shortly thereafter she hired a certain Wayne to manage her farm. He had come to Oregon with a criminal record, so assumed a new name. From June, 1972 until Sophia's death in November, 1973, Sophia and Wayne occupied the house on the farm. At the time, Sophia was 77 years old, in poor health, and suffering from various physical disabilities, but apparently mentally sharp and strongwilled. Eventually, Sophia signed a new will naming Wayne as sole beneficiary. The court held that Wayne had exercised undue influence over Sophia, and held the new will invalid. The new will was prepared by a friend of Wayne's, who had also come from California and had a criminal record too. The court found the following factors present, which indicated improper influence by Wayne:

(a) Procurement

Wayne, as beneficiary, participated in the preparation of the will by providing his friend with the description of the farm, arranging for his friend to type the will, and also arranging for the witnesses to the will.

(b) Lack of independent advice

Sophia did not have any independent advice from her own attorney or other persons.

(c) Secrecy and haste

Apparently one reason why no lawyer was engaged to prepare the will, according to the court, was Wayne's desire to keep it a secret. There was also evidence that there was considerable haste in the preparation of the will, which was signed four days before Sophia's death.

(d) Change in attitude toward others

It was significant to the court that Sophia was disinheriting one of her daughters, obviously reflecting displeasure with her, which the court felt was probably caused by Wayne.

(e) Unnatural gift

Although it is possible to make an eccentric gift, nevertheless, the circumstances will be weighed in determining whether undue influences existed. In this case, when coupled with other facts, undue influence was indicated. It was certainly an unnatural thing to give everything to a handyman in lieu of a daughter.

(f) Susceptibility to influence

Finally, the court found that although Sophia was strong-willed, she was very susceptible to influence because of her dependence on Wayne as a result of her physical infirmities.

d. SIGNING YOUR WILL

The formal requirements for a valid will in Oregon are very simple. However, to prevent a claim of undue influence or lack of testamentary capacity, you should also take the following precautions.

1. Read the will

Be sure that you have read your will carefully and that it says precisely what you want it to say. If you do not understand any provision, have it explained to you and satisfy yourself that that is what you want in your will. After all, your will is one of the most personal legal documents you will ever sign.

2. Take your time

Do not make any decision in haste that you may later regret. It can be dangerous to have a quick, simple will prepared just before you go on vacation, assuming that it will be a temporary measure until you return. You should always plan your will as if you were going to die the next day.

3. Stay calm and alert

Some people use their will to punish someone for past injuries or insults. There is nothing illegal about using your will for such purposes, but if you sign your will in haste and anger, you run the risk of having it contested.

Try to avoid taking any medication that might affect your alertness when you sign your will. Sometimes there is no way of avoiding signing a will while in the hospital, but hospital and deathbed wills are tempting targets for disinherited heirs.

4. Objective witnesses

When you sign your will, do not have anyone present who is named as a devisee or beneficiary in the will. Although a beneficiary may be a witness, it is wise to use other people. Don't give anyone a chance to claim undue influence.

5. The formal requirements

The most common way to make your will is for you to sign it in the presence of two or more witnesses. The witnesses must see you sign the will, then, in turn, "attest" the will by signing their names to it. But there are no requirements that you ask the witnesses to sign the will or that the witnesses sign in your presence or that they sign in the presence of each other. There is also no requirement for you to publish your will (i.e., announce to the witnesses that the document is your will).

A typical testimonium clause, which is the clause that states you have signed your will, might be as follows:

> I have signed this will in Multnomah County, Oregon, on May 3, 199-, by signing my name on this page of my will, which consists of four pages, including this page and excluding the affidavit on the following page.

The clause preceding the signatures of the witnesses is called the attestation clause and might read as follows:

> The foregoing will was signed by John Doe, the testator in our presence, and we have signed our names as witnesses in Multnomah County, Oregon, on May 3, 199-.

See the example of a will in Sample #2.

There are two additional ways to make a will in Oregon:

(a) Instead of signing the will yourself, you may direct one of the witnesses to sign your name for you. That person should also sign his or her own name and acknowledge that the direction was received from the testator. This method would be appropriate if you had some infirmity which made it difficult for you to sign your name.

(b) You may sign your name outside the presence of the two witnesses, and then acknowledge your signature to the two witnesses when they sign. The witnesses must hear you acknowledge your signature, then sign it themselves.

A will must be in writing, but there is no requirement that it be typed. It could be handwritten or printed. You should date it and initial or sign each page, and sign the last page in full. If you have copies made of your will, be sure that you only sign the original. If you sign two copies, and only one is found at your death, it may be presumed that you revoked your will by destroying the missing copy. This could invalidate the signed copy, even if you intended it to be your valid will.

A will does not have to be notarized, but it has become common practice to attach a separate affidavit to the will, signed by the witnesses (but not the testator) and notarized, stating that they witnessed the will and that the testator appeared to be of sound mind and over the age of 18.

SAMPLE #2
A SIMPLE WILL

WILL OF JOHN SMITH

1. DECLARATION. I, John Smith, declare this my will and revoke all prior wills and codicils. I am a resident of Multnomah County, Oregon, my Social Security number is 000-00-0000, and I was born January 1, 1950.

2. HEIRS. I am married to Mary Smith. We have three children, John Smith, Jr., who is of legal age, Sarah Smith, born April 10, 1985, and George Smith, born February 14, 1989. Any reference in my will to my children includes not only the children listed herein but also any afterborn or adopted children of mine.

3. PERSONAL REPRESENTATIVE. I name as personal representative, to serve without bond, my wife, Mary Smith. If she fails to qualify, or having qualified, ceases to serve, I name Oregon American National Bank as my personal representative.

4. DISPOSITION OF PROPERTY. I give all my property to my wife, Mary Smith. If she fails to survive me, I give all my property, in equal shares, to my children surviving me, and by right of representation, to the issue surviving me of each of my children predeceasing me. If all my children predecease me, leaving no issue surviving me, I give fifty percent (50%) of the value of my estate to my heirs at law and fifty percent (50%) of the value of my estate to those persons who would have been my wife's heirs at law had she died at the time of my death.

5. GUARDIAN. If my wife fails to survive me, I direct that my friends, Ronald and Joyce Peterson, be appointed guardians of any of my children surviving me who are under the age of majority at the time of my death.

SAMPLE #2 — Continued

6. SURVIVORSHIP. No person named in my will shall be deemed to have survived me unless living on the thirtieth (30th) day after the date of my death.

I have signed this will in Multnomah County, Oregon, on May 3, 199-, by signing my name on this page of my will, which consists of two pages, including this page and excluding the affidavit on the following page.

John Smith

The foregoing was signed by John Smith, the testator in our presence, and we have signed our names as witnesses in Multnomah County, Oregon on May 3, 199-.

I M Witness

U R Witness

Usually, this affidavit is all that is required to have the will admitted to probate. This is known as a "self-proving" will. The advantage of having the affidavit signed at the time the will is signed is that it avoids having to locate the witnesses at the testator's death, which may be many years later.

No physical disability, such as a visual or hearing impairment, bars a person who has testamentary capacity from making a will. For example, in an early Oregon court decision, the will of a 74-year-old speechless paralytic was challenged. He had testamentary capacity and disposed of his property in his will by giving negative and affirmative replies to questions asked of him. After the will had been written, it was read to him item by item and his assent was given by nodding his head. The will was valid.

There are two types of wills that are invalid in Oregon:

(a) A holographic will, or a will that is handwritten, dated, and signed by you but not witnessed. All wills must be witnessed to be valid.

(b) A nuncupative will, or an oral will, where you declare or dictate your will before a certain number of witnesses, and it is afterwards put in writing but not signed.

e. HOW A WILL IS REVOKED

1. Marriage

If you marry after you make your will, your marriage automatically revokes your will if you die and your spouse survives you. There are two exceptions to this rule.

(a) If the will indicates an intent that it not be revoked by a subsequent marriage or that it was drafted under circumstances establishing that it was in contemplation of the marriage, then it will not be deemed revoked. An example of this might be where you are contemplating marriage and want to be sure your will is in order before your wedding. This might be done by a provision in the will which reads:

> I am presently engaged to be married to John Smith. I make this will expressly in contemplation of my marriage to him, and I intend that it not be revoked by such a marriage.

(b) If you and your spouse entered into a contract before the marriage that either makes a provision for the spouse or provides that the spouse shall have no rights in your estate, then the will is not revoked by the marriage. This might happen where both spouses are entering second marriages and they want to make sure their respective estates are protected for their own children. It is not unusual to enter into a prenuptial or premarital agreement to make those provisions. In this case, a will made prior to marriage would be consistent with such an agreement and would not be revoked by the marriage. Such agreements are discussed in chapter 11.

2. By annulment or divorce

A court decree annulling or dissolving a marriage automatically revokes the portions of a will in favor of the former spouse, including a provision naming a former spouse the personal representative. This is done by treating the former spouse as if he or she did not survive the testator. The remainder of the will would still be valid.

A provision could be placed in the will stating that the will was made in contemplation of the annulment or marriage dissolution and that the former spouse is to receive his or her share under the will, or act as personal representative in spite of the decree dissolving or annulling the marriage. In that case the subsequent annulment or marriage dissolution would not bar the former spouse from taking his or her share under the will.

There must be a court decree before the spouse is barred from receiving his or her share under a will. This means that if a spouse dies while an annulment or marriage dissolution proceeding is pending but before a decree is entered, the surviving spouse would be entitled to inherit under the deceased spouse's will.

3. By a new will

A will is revoked by signing a new will, provided either that the new will expressly revokes the prior will or, even without such language, that the new will disposes of all your property. A typical provision in a new will might read "I revoke all prior wills and codicils." If a new will does not replace the old will but merely amends it, it is known as a "codicil" and does not revoke the will.

4. By destruction

You can revoke your will simply by tearing it up and throwing it away, provided that you intend to revoke it by such act. In order for the physical destruction of a will to constitute a valid revocation, you must have the same testamentary capacity and freedom from undue influence that is necessary to make a will. If someone influences you to tear up your will, such revocation is not valid.

You cannot partially revoke your will or amend your will by cutting out portions of it or writing over portions of it. It is an all or nothing proposition. If you intend to revoke your will or to amend it, do not write on it. If you want to change it, see your attorney and have a new will or a codicil made. If you do intend to revoke your will in its entirety and do not want a new will, then tear it up, burn it, or destroy it so that there is no question of your intent. Otherwise, whatever you intended very possibly will not be fulfilled and will probably lead to litigation. Either the entire will is considered revoked, or the entire will is considered valid. Partial revocation is not possible.

For example, Nellie made pen and pencil marks on 17 of the 22 paragraphs in her will. The court held that she intended to revoke her will and held it invalid.

In another case, Ella cut out or crossed through various paragraphs of her will. There was testimony at a trial that she wanted to give her estate to various religious and charitable organizations and was crossing out or excluding just her relatives. But the court held that she intended to revoke her entire will, so her estate went to her relatives instead of to the charities.

In another case, Charles attempted to cancel out certain paragraphs of his will by drawing lines through those paragraphs with his pen and writing that he was canceling them. He also wrote in three additions to the will. The court held that there can be no partial revocation and held the will valid and admitted it to probate, even though his intent was clear that he wanted to make the changes indicated.

f. AGREEMENTS CONCERNING WILLS

It is possible to make a binding contract with another person relating to your will. For example, you could agree to —

(a) make your will in a certain way,

(b) give or devise certain property to a person,

(c) not revoke or change your will or devise, or

(d) die intestate; in other words, contract not to make a will.

If you breach the contract, the other person can sue you or your estate.

A typical situation where such an agreement is made is a contract between married couples — particularly in second marriages where the spouses want to protect the children of the first marriage (see chapter 11). Another common contract is a promise to devise in exchange for services rendered.

An earlier practice was for a married couple to write both their wills in one document. This is known as a joint, mutual, or reciprocal will.

For joint wills executed after January 1, 1974, a special law provides that the writing of a joint will does not create a presumption of a contract not to revoke the will after the death of one of the spouses. Any contract relating to a will made after January 1, 1974 must be indicated in writing either in —

(a) provisions of a will stating the material provisions of the contract, or

(b) an express reference in a will to a contract and evidence outside the will proving the terms of the contract, or

(c) a written statement signed by the deceased evidencing the contract.

g. WILLS SIGNED IN OTHER STATES

What if you signed a will while a resident in another state and then moved to Oregon? Your will is still valid in Oregon, provided that it is signed and complies with the formalities of the state where you resided at the time you signed it or, if you signed it in a state other than the state of your residence, it complies with the formalities of the state where you signed it.

Nevertheless, if you move to Oregon from another state, you should have a new will drafted by an Oregon attorney, partly because there will be matters of Oregon law other than the formalities of signing that may require different provisions in your will, and partly because, upon your death, it may be easier to prove your will by Oregon witnesses.

If you sign a will in Oregon and then move to another state, your Oregon will may or may not be valid in that state, depending on that state's laws. You should therefore have a new will drawn up by an attorney in the state to which you move.

h. WHERE TO KEEP YOUR WILL

There is no government agency in Oregon that will store your will for you while you are alive. Consider storing your will in one of the locations described below.

1. Safe deposit box

A safe deposit box at a financial institution is the best place to keep your will. This is the place where there is the least risk that your will can be destroyed by fire or other natural disaster, lost, stolen or misplaced.

It is the most customary place to keep a will, and, therefore, the most likely place to look for your will after your death.

2. Trust department

If you name a bank as first or second choice of personal representative or as trustee in your will, the trust departments of most banks will store your will for you at no cost as a courtesy to you.

3. At home

Many people prefer storing their wills at home. If this is your preference, you should keep it in a fireproof safe or file, or, if you do not have one, then in some other relatively fireproof location, such as your freezer (in a waterproof container).

4. Attorney's office

Many attorneys store their client's wills for them in their office safe deposit box. You should give this alternative careful thought before selecting it. It may be difficult for you to ask the attorney for your will if you later want to change attorneys. Also, the personal representative should have the option to choose an attorney to help probate your estate after you die. He or she may feel pressured to use the attorney who is storing your will. Even if there is a provision in your will that directs the personal representative to hire a particular attorney, the personal representative is not bound to do so.

If an attorney stores your will and he or she dies, retires, leaves the practice of law, or moves out of state, it may be difficult for you or your personal representative to locate your will.

5. With other people

Some people prefer their personal representative or some close relative to store their will. This is not a problem if the personal representative is a financial institution. But if you name an individual and that person keeps it at home, there is always the risk of fire, theft, and misplacement. Also, if the individual stores your will in a safe deposit box and dies before you do, the contents of your will may be disclosed to strangers.

Whether you store your will in your safe deposit box, your bank's trust department, or elsewhere, make sure it can be located after your death. If your will can't be found after your death, there is a good chance that it will not be admitted to probate and will not control the disposition of your probate property.

You can improve the chances of your will being found by —

(a) keeping a copy of your will at home with your other important papers and noting the location of the original,

(b) noting the location of the will in a letter of instructions,

(c) informing your personal representative of the location of the will or the location of the letter of instructions,

(d) having your personal representative as a co-lessee of the safe deposit box, and

(e) informing relatives, friends, or clergy either of the location of the will or of the letter of instructions.

i. LETTER OF INSTRUCTIONS

One of the main reasons for the sometimes lengthy delay in starting probate procedure is the disarray in which most people leave their property and financial affairs. This delay can cause unnecessary expense to the estate by allowing defaults on obligations to creditors and extra interest and service charges. It may also lead to hardship for persons who were dependent on the decedent for support.

You can minimize these risks by organizing your personal and financial affairs, both for yourself and for your personal representative, with the preparation of a letter of instructions. This could contain the following:

(a) A list of all your property and debts (see chapter 1)

(b) The location of all important documents relating to your estate, such as your will, life insurance policies, pension, documents, etc.

(c) The location of your safe deposit box

(d) The names, addresses, and telephone numbers of your professional advisors, including your accountant, attorney, life insurance agent, stock broker, trust officer, or financial counselor (If you want your personal representative to use the services of these particular advisors, note this in your letter, not in your will.)

(e) Instructions concerning your funeral, burial, or cremation wishes (You may want to indicate what friends, relatives, or organizations should be contacted at your death, particularly if they live out of town and may not hear about your death right away.)

(f) The names, addresses, and relationships of those relatives who would have been your heirs had you died without a will, and the dates of birth of any minor heirs (This information will be necessary for your personal representative to have immediately at your death.)

(g) The names and addresses of all devisees under your will or beneficiaries under any trust agreement if they are not heirs

(h) Your birth date, place of birth, social security number, and the names of your father and mother (including mother's maiden name) and whether or not you are a veteran

(i) Special instructions to your personal representative telling him or her how to divide up your furniture or other tangible property and the reasons for omitting an heir from your will (This will serve only as a guide; it will not be binding.)

(j) Once you have completed, dated, and signed your letter of instructions, you should put one copy with your original will, keep another copy with a copy of your will at home in a place that is easy to find after your death, and give one copy (in a sealed envelope to ensure confidentiality) to your personal representative, your attorney, and any other close personal advisor. As an alternative, give them a letter, to be opened at your death, telling them where to find your letter of instructions.

j. REVIEW YOUR WILL AND ESTATE PLAN

Once you have your will, you should not put it away and forget about it for the next 20 years. A will can become outdated because of changes in your marital status, the death of a beneficiary, a substantial increase or decrease in the size of your estate, a move to another state or country, or a change in the law. It's a good idea to review all your documents, your financial inventory, and your letter of instructions once a year or on some other regular basis.

k. SAFE DEPOSIT BOXES

A safe deposit box at a bank is the best place to store your will and other important documents that may be hard to replace like birth and marriage certificates.

Many people believe that a person's safe deposit box is "frozen" after a person dies. This is not true in Oregon. If a safe deposit box to which a deceased person had access is jointly rented, the surviving joint renter has the right to remove the contents.

The situation becomes more complicated, however, if the deceased person is the sole renter of the box. Normally the personal representative is the only person who has a right to take possession of a deceased's property. Who is entitled to act as personal representative, of course, depends on the terms of the deceased's will, and frequently that will is in the safe deposit box. Also, there may be no way of knowing whether probate is necessary until the box is examined. Obviously, therefore, the bank or savings and loan association where the box is located must have some discretion in determining who is entitled to access of the box when the sole renter dies.

Although practices vary from institution to institution, generally one of three policies is followed.

1. Reasonable basis

Any person who has a key and who has some reasonable basis for gaining access to the box (such as a close family member) will be permitted to examine the contents of the box in the presence of an officer from the financial institution. This will disclose whether there is a will in the box and also whether or not there are sufficient assets to require probate of the person's estate.

2. Attorney

If there is a will in the box, the financial institution will permit it to be released to the attorney who prepared the will, but will not turn it over to the personal representative named in the will or some other family member.

3. Personal representative

The financial institution will not permit release of any contents of the box other than the will, except to a duly appointed personal representative or, if there is a small estate affidavit filed, then to the so-called "claiming successors."

There will be occasions when a financial institution will not permit access or removal of a will or any other contents without a court order, for instance, if there are competing factions of a family demanding access or release of the contents. There are several drawbacks to leaving a safe deposit box in your sole name. For instance, the financial institution may inadvertently permit certain family members to have access to the box which would not be consistent with your desires. On the other hand, a person you assumed would have all rights to deal with your affairs may suddenly discover that the financial institution is barring access to the box.

As another example, the typical policy of releasing a will solely to the attorney who prepared it and not to the personal representative named in the will is not in accord with Oregon law. The personal representative is entitled to select his or her own attorney and is not required to retain the attorney who prepared the will. That attorney, therefore, has no legal interest or right to the deceased person's will.

Oregon law also says that a person having custody of a will must deliver the will to the probate court or to the personal representative within 30 days after receiving information that the testator is dead.

If you do not have a spouse or close relative, name your personal representative as a co-renter of the box.

9
PLANNING YOUR WILL

Your right to dispose of your property at death is a valuable incident of ownership. This has been described by Oregon's courts as a "sacred and inviolable" right of your absolute dominion over your property. As part of that right, you are entitled to give your property to whomever you please and without regard to the natural or legitimate claims of your heirs. While you cannot totally disinherit a spouse under Oregon law, you can favor your lover over your spouse and give your lover more than your spouse, or you can completely disinherit a child, and this in no way makes your will invalid. There is no "reasonably prudent man's standard" as is applied in other areas of law. As one Oregon court has stated:

> No man is bound to make a will in such a manner as to deserve approbation from the prudent, the wise, or the good. A testator is permitted to be capricious, improvident, and is, moreover, at liberty to conceal the circumstances and the motives by which he has been actuated in his deposition.

Whether or not you exercise your right is up to you. If you do not exercise your right, then the state exercises that right for you and disposes of your property at death as outlined in chapter 7. You should always plan your will as if you were going to die tomorrow. If you do not treat your will and estate planning that way, then, in effect, the state of Oregon will do it for you.

A will must reflect your intentions very clearly, because when the question of your intent becomes important, you are no longer around to explain to anyone what you meant. A good will is not only clear and precise, it also tries to cover the various contingencies that can occur between the time you sign the will and the time of your death. It is particularly important that the will cover the possibility that one or more of the beneficiaries you designate in your will may die before you do, or that property that you specifically mention in your will is no longer owned by you at your death.

a. THE OPENING CLAUSE

A simple opening clause might read:

> I, JOHN SMITH, declare this my will and revoke all prior wills and codicils. I am a resident of Multnomah County, Oregon, my social security number is 000-00-0000, and I was born January 1, 1950.

This clause serves several functions.

(a) It indicates that you intend the document to be your will. You do not need to say "last will and testament." You do not have to state that you are of sound and disposing mind, which is common in many wills. Such a statement does not prove that in fact you are of sound and disposing mind. There are better ways of showing that.

(b) It is important to revoke expressly all prior wills and codicils. You should do so even if you do not remember ever having signed a will before. You may have forgotten that you did. Of course, if you are amending a prior will rather than redoing it entirely, such language would be inappropriate.

(c) You should declare that you are a resident of the state of Oregon. Your residence is the place you consider your "real" home or domicile. The laws of the state of your residence determine how your will is interpreted and how your estate is taxed.

b. YOUR HEIRS

An heirship clause in a will might read:

> On the date of my will, my only heirs are my wife, Mary Smith, and our three children, John Smith, Jr., who is of legal age, Sarah Smith, born April 10, 1985, and George Smith, born February 14, 1989.

An heirship clause serves several purposes.

(a) Naming your heirs in your will is a good way of showing that you had testamentary capacity when you signed your will. Be sure you are accurate; if you make mistakes identifying your heirs, that might suggest you lack testamentary capacity.

(b) An heirship clause is also helpful to your personal representative, who must notify all your heirs that you have died and your will has been admitted to probate.

(c) If you have children, listing them in your will will help your personal representative decide whether or not you intentionally or accidentally omitted any child born to you or adopted by you after you sign your will. Such children are known as "pretermitted children." The basic rules about these children are as follows:

  (i) If you have one or more children at the time of signing your will and make no provision in your will for your children, then an afterborn or adopted child would not be included in your will.

  (ii) If you do have children at the time you sign the will and make provisions for them in your will, then any afterborn or adopted child would be entitled to share equally in the gift to your children.

(iii) If you have no children at the time you sign the will, and thereafter a child is born to or adopted by you, then that child is entitled to the share which it would be entitled to under the laws of intestate succession. This rule does not include stepchildren or foster children.

(d) Listing the dates of birth of children is helpful when they are minors, since this will indicate to the personal representative whether such children are minors at the time of your death and may need a conservator. It is also helpful if you establish a trust for your children which provides that they are to receive their share of the trust at a certain age, say 25.

(e) If you intend to disinherit an heir, it is a good idea to name the heir and state your intention. This way, there can be no question about your intent and no basis for the claim that you "just forgot" about a particular heir. You might add the words "I expressly make no provision in my will for my son, Charles."

If you want to explain the reasons for the disinheritance, do it in a letter to the heir. This way your reasons do not become part of the public record when your will is admitted to probate.

There is a common misconception that you must leave one dollar to each heir you disinherit. This is not true. It will only cause complications for your personal representative, who will have to treat that heir as a devisee under your will and give the heir notice to which he or she would not otherwise be entitled.

There are two exceptions to the rule that you can disinherit all your heirs:

(i) You may partially, but not totally, disinherit your spouse.

(ii) Your spouse and dependent children are entitled to support from your estate during probate. Even disinherited children are entitled to support during probate if they are dependents. This could last up to two years and possibly use up all your probate property.

c. PERSONAL REPRESENTATIVE

The personal representative is the person you name in your will to handle the administration of your estate when you die. It can be an individual such as a close relative, a trusted advisor such as your attorney or accountant, or a bank with trust powers. Banks authorized to engage in trust business in Oregon are listed in the Appendix.

Individuals who are not qualified to act as a personal representative include incompetents, persons under age 18, persons who have been suspended for misconduct or disbarred from the practice of law during the period of such suspension or disbarment, persons who have resigned from the Oregon State Bar when charges of professional misconduct or disciplinary proceedings are pending, and judges of Oregon courts. Even a convicted felon may act as a personal representative unless the court finds that the reasons for his or her conviction are similar grounds for removal of a personal representative.

Select your personal representative like your trustee (see chapter 5). You will want to consider qualities of professional management, impartiality, perpetual existence, integrity, solvency, and cost. However, several unique factors need to be considered in choosing a personal representative.

(a) Financial institutions with trust powers are in the business of settling estates and generally do a more competent job than an individual. They are not required to file a personal representative's bond. A financial institution, of course, will take its statutory fee for acting as personal representative and will seek additional fees for extraordinary services. Attorney fees should be lower than in an estate where an inexperienced individual acts as personal representative because the bank will do many things for its statutory fee that an attorney would charge for if an individual were the personal representative. On the other hand, frequently an individual personal representative who is also a beneficiary under the will will waive the personal representative fee.

(b) You may name two or more personal representatives. For instance, if you have two children and you want to treat them equally for all purposes under your will, you could name them both as personal representatives. Another reason is to ensure adequate professional attention to the administration of your estate. Naming two personal representatives may make administration of an estate more cumbersome, however, because all steps require the concurrence of both.

(c) You may name a personal representative who is a beneficiary under the will. In a husband-wife situation, the surviving spouse is the logical choice. He or she will normally work very closely with and be advised by the attorney.

(d) You can name your attorney. However, there are many chores of the personal representative, such as cleaning out a house and getting it ready for sale, or getting all the personal property together, or paying routine bills, that do not require a lawyer's expertise or justify a lawyer's fee. It may thus be cheaper in the long run for you to let the attorney act solely as attorney for the personal representative and select some other person whose hourly rate is not as high.

(e) Wills commonly provide that a personal representative is not required to serve with bond. Without such a provision, the personal representative is required to have a bond, and it frequently must be a commercial surety bond. Such bonds have an annual premium calculated at the rate of about $4 per $1,000 of value of assets. Thus, a $50,000 estate might require a bond costing $200 or more per year. If you trust an individual enough to ask that individual to be your personal representative, you had better trust him or her enough to serve without bond. Otherwise, name a bank as your personal representative.

(f) Always name one or more alternative personal representatives in case your first choice dies before you or for some other reason fails to qualify or ceases to serve. This is especially important if you are naming an individual rather than a bank as your personal representative, but it is also advisable where you name a bank as first choice. Sometimes a bank may decline to serve. You may wish to name an individual as first choice and a bank second choice.

d. WHEN YOU OWN REAL PROPERTY IN ANOTHER STATE

If you are an Oregon resident with real property in another state, your estate might require a separate probate in the other state. This is called "ancillary administration." This would ensure that such real property is distributed according to your will. Your intangible personal property, wherever located, and your real tangible personal property located in Oregon, would be probated by an Oregon probate court. You should make certain that your Oregon personal representative can act in the state where your real property is located. If not, name a second personal representative, and make sure that your will complies with the laws of the state where such real property is located.

e. HOW TO MAKE GIFTS IN YOUR WILL

There are three types of gifts of property in a will: specific devise, general devise, and residue.

1. Specific devise

A specific devise is a devise of a specific thing or specific part of your estate. For instance, if you give your rings and jewelry, or your house, or the balance in your savings account to a certain person or charity, such gifts are specific devises.

2. General devise

A general devise is a devise chargeable generally on your estate or property. Thus if you give a gift of $1,000 to someone, this means that you do not care where it comes from in your estate, as long as that person gets the $1,000.

This may be contrasted, for example, with a specific devise in which you give whatever funds are in your checking account at the time of your death. Such a gift would constitute a specific devise. Generally, because of the way that checking and savings accounts can fluctuate, it is better to give a specific dollar amount rather than the balance in some account to a person.

3. Residue

The residue of your estate is all your probate property except property that constitutes a general or specific devise. The clause disposing of the residue of your estate may be the most important clause in your will.

You do not need to make specific or general devises. For example, your will could say only "I give all my estate in equal shares to my children."

However, if you do not have a clause disposing of the residue of your estate (or all of your estate if you have no specific or general devises), then the probate property you do not mention and specifically devise in your will will be distributed to your heirs according to the laws of intestate succession.

Because you cannot predict what probate property you will own at your death, it is important to use the terms "residue" or "residuary estate," rather than trying to list every item of probate property you own in your residuary clause. The term "residue" gives you absolute assurance that none of your probate property will go by intestate succession.

You may give the residue of your estate in equal shares or list it by percentages. For instance, if you want to distribute it in unequal shares you might give 50% of the residue to one child, 25% to another child, and 12½% to two grandchildren. In this way, you will ensure that distribution will be made in terms of the value of your assets and property at the time of your death and that you will dispose of everything.

A simple will containing all three types of devises might read as follows:

(a) I give my house and my car to my son, Michael. (A specific devise.)

(b) I give the sum of $50,000 to my daughter, Alice. (A general devise.)

(c) I give the residue to my daughter, Barbara.

f. PLANNING SPECIFIC AND GENERAL DEVISES

Specific devises and general devises require special planning. For example, if you give all your probate property in equal shares to your children, it doesn't normally matter how you allocate funeral expenses, taxes, or administration expenses. When the estate is settled, each child will get an equal share of what is left. But if you give specific or general devises, planning becomes a little more complicated.

These are some of the things you should consider:

(a) What happens if you sell your house on contract after you sign the will but it has not been paid off when you die? Who gets the balance due on the contract?

(b) Who gets insurance proceeds if the house is destroyed by fire?

(c) Who pays the mortgage? The funeral bill? The debts and administration costs?

(d) Who gets the income from the house during probate?

Careful planning can cover each of these areas in your will. However, if you do not plan, specific rules will determine what happens.

g. WHAT IF PROPERTY IS SOLD OR DESTROYED?

If you specifically devise property to someone, and you sell it before you die, the specific devise fails, and the devisee gets neither the property nor its equivalent value. This is known as the doctrine of ademption by extinction. Simply put, you cannot give away in your will what you do not own at your death.

A special statute, however, modifies this rule by providing for "nonademption" of specific devises in certain situations. In these situations, the property does not "adeem" and the devisee still gets something.

1. Insured property

If specifically devised property is destroyed or damaged, and it is insured, the specific devisee is entitled to any insurance proceeds paid to your personal representative after your death, together with a cash payment, equal to the amount of insurance proceeds that you received during the six months preceding your death. If the property is not insured, the devise fails.

2. **Sale of property**

If you sell specifically devised real property under a land sales contract, the specific devisee gets title to the property. This is subject to a contractual obligation to convey title to the buyer when the buyer pays off the contract. In effect, the specific devisee receives the right to collect the balance due on the contract and a security interest in the property.

If you sell specifically devised real property by any other method or if you sell personal property, the specific devisee is entitled to the balance of the purchase price unpaid at death, any interest accrued but unpaid at death, any security interest in the property securing the obligation, and a general pecuniary devise equal to the amount of the purchase price paid to you within six months before your death.

If a guardian or conservator is appointed for you and sells specifically devised property or receives insurance proceeds or a condemnation award relating to such property, the specific devisee is entitled to the proceeds from such sale, the insurance proceeds, or the condemnation award.

3. **Condemnation**

If specifically devised property is taken by condemnation before your death, the specific devisee is entitled to the amount of the condemnation award unpaid at your death plus a general pecuniary devise equal to the amount of the award paid to you during the six months prior to your death. Your property is condemned when the state or other governmental agency forces you to sell your property to it for some public purpose such as a highway or park.

4. **Stocks and bonds**

If you specifically devise stocks, bonds, or other securities, and receive additional shares after the date of your will, the specific devise is considered to include the additional or substituted securities.

h. MORTGAGES AND OTHER ENCUMBRANCES

A mortgage is just one of a variety of encumbrances that can exist against property. An encumbrance is any claim against the property that shows up on the chain of title and represents an obligation to some person, organization, or government agency. The law divides encumbrances into two categories:

(a) Voluntary encumbrances including mortgages, trust deeds, security agreements, pledges, public improvement assessment liens, or contract liens

(b) Involuntary encumbrances including judgments and tax liens

The specific devisee must assume and pay any voluntary encumbrances, but the residuary devisees will have to pay any involuntary encumbrances.

A specific devisee has two options with a voluntary encumbrance:

(a) Require the personal representative to apply any rents or profits received from the property to the encumbrance

(b) Request the personal representative to satisfy the encumbrance out of specifically devised property

You may modify these rules by directing that the specifically devised property be given free and clear of any encumbrances.

i. WHO PAYS THE BILLS?

There are several expenses that must be paid after a person's death and during the administration of an estate. The principal ones are the following:

(a) Debt owed by the deceased as of the date of death including expenses of last illness and income taxes

(b) Funeral expenses, attorney and personal representative fees, court costs, and other administration expenses

(c) Expenses relating to a specific devise, such as mortgage payments, property taxes, and repairs on a house

(d) Inheritance or estate taxes (death taxes)

The personal representative is not required to make any payments on a mortgage or other voluntary encumbrances except from rents and profits received from the property. Property taxes and repairs are first paid out of the income from the property. Any excess is treated like any other administration expense.

Debts of the deceased and funeral and administration expenses are paid out of property in the following order:

(a) Property not disposed of by the will (This will rarely happen if a person has a will. It means that the person would have had to die partially intestate with part of the probate property going to the heirs)

(b) Out of the residue

(c) Out of the general devises

(d) Out of the specific devises

This is called the order of abatement. Abatement is proportionate within each class of devise. For example, if you provide that one-half of the residue goes to each of two different persons, then each person's share of the residue is abated to the extent of one-half of such expenses.

These rules apply regardless of any provision in your will directing your personal representative to pay your "just debts." By law, your personal representative is required to pay your legal obligations and the expenses of administration. If you include directions in your will for your personal representative to pay your debts, it will just cause confusion.

j. WHO PAYS DEATH TAXES?

Inheritance and estate taxes are apportioned among all devisees in proportion to the value of their interests in the estate.

Death taxes are also apportioned among probate and nonprobate property. For example, if you died owning life insurance and jointly owned property plus probate property, the beneficiary of the insurance policy and the surviving joint owner would each have to pay a proportionate share of the death taxes. Normally, the personal representative files the death tax return, and nonprobate property owners pay their share of the death taxes to the personal representative.

This rule can be changed by a provision in your will directing that death taxes be paid out of a certain part of your estate, typically the residue. This may be important if you make specific devises and want to make sure that such devisees get the property undiminished by death taxes. For instance, in the example in section **e.**, Michael would have to come up with funds to pay his share of the death taxes on the house and car, and Alice's $50,000 gift would be reduced by its share of death taxes unless you had a tax apportionment clause which said the all death taxes on probate property are to be paid out of the residue. A typical clause might read as follows:

> Death Taxes: My personal representative shall pay all estate, inheritance, succession, and transfer taxes, plus interest and penalties (death taxes), which become payable by reason of my death in respect of any property passing under my will, out of the residue of my estate as an expense of administration and without apportionment and shall not prorate or charge them against any specific or general devises under my will. Death taxes on property passing outside my will shall be apportioned in the manner provided by law.

k. WHO GETS THE INCOME DURING PROBATE?

The administration of an estate in Oregon will take six months to more than two years. Who gets the income from the probate property during that period of time?

The income is not used to pay expenses in settling the estate, such as debts, funeral expenses, and administration expenses. Those are a charge against the probate property. Specific devisees are entitled to the income from the property devised to them less taxes, ordinary repairs, and other expenses of operation and management of the property.

General pecuniary devisees do not share in the income during probate. But if they are not paid within one year after the personal representative is appointed, they are entitled to 5% interest on the devise, to be paid out of the residue. The residuary devisees receive all the other income.

l. YOUR TANGIBLE PERSONAL PROPERTY

If you are giving your furniture, furnishings, personal belongings and other tangible personal property to more than one person, you may find it cumbersome to list every piece of property and figure out who shall get it. You may also change your mind or give it away or buy additional personal property so that the list quickly becomes outdated.

There are several ways to handle this problem. For instance, if you are giving it to all your children, and they are old enough to make their own choice, you can provide that they may divide it among themselves as they may mutually agree, but if they cannot agree within some time period, for instance 90 days, then the personal representative shall decide how to divide it. There are several other ways to handle this, particularly if your children are minors and you are covering the contingency that your spouse has died before you. You can do one of the following:

(a) Direct the personal representative to divide the tangible personal property among your children in as nearly equal shares as possible in terms of value, taking into account whatever wishes each child expresses for a particular item.

(b) You could do the same as in the first proposal, except that you give the personal representative a list of how you would like to see it divided among your children. You might also say in your will that you know the personal representative will distribute the property in accordance with your wishes. This would be considered "precatory," which means that your wishes are not legally binding, but that you are trusting your personal representative to distribute it as you wish. The benefit of this arrangement is that you can update your list from time to time without having to redo your will.

(c) You could give all your tangible personal property to a close friend or relative with precatory language similar to the above proposal. Such a clause might be appropriate where the personal representative is a bank or a person who would not be aware of your desires or understand or know your children well enough to make a reasonable division of the personal property.

(d) If you want a legally binding direction for distribution of specific items of personal property, but do not want to incorporate or include the entire list in your will, you can incorporate a list by reference. However, the list of personal property must be dated and in existence prior to the date of the will to make it binding on the personal representative. If you intend later to update the list, then you will have to re-execute the will to make the list binding.

m. WHAT IF A DEVISEE DIES BEFORE YOU DO?

In Oregon, if a devisee dies before the testator and that person is related by blood or adoption to the testator and, in addition, leaves lineal descendants, then the descendants take the devisee's gift by representation. Thus, if you make a gift of $1,000 to a sister, and she dies before you do, leaving two children of her own, each child would get $500. If there are no descendants, the gift would lapse and become a part of the residue. This is known as the antilapse law.

This law will give you some protection to cover such a contingency, providing that you are giving property to relatives and that this reflects your desires. However, it is better for you to provide specifically for disposition of your property in case one or more of your devisees die before you do.

To a certain extent, you have to play the odds in this situation. For instance, if you have two or more children and they have children of their own, there is little likelihood that all your children and grandchildren will die before both you and your spouse. Generally most people desire that if a child dies before they do, that child's share will go by representation to his or her children, or their grandchildren. If, as is sometimes the case, you want your child's spouse to receive the property, then you must expressly provide for this in your will.

Another common occurrence is where a couple has only one child. Suppose that child died before both you and your spouse and had no children, and you made no provision in your will for such a contingency. What would happen to your estate? It would depend on the accident of who died first: you or your spouse.

If you died first, and then your spouse died, leaving no children and with no other provision in his or her will, then all the estate would go to his or her heirs at law, which would be the parents if living, otherwise to brothers and sisters or other heirs. If he or she died before you did, then everything would go to your heirs at law upon your subsequent death.

Thus, it may be appropriate to provide that if such a situation were to occur, one-half of the estate would go to your side of the family and one-half to your spouse's side of the family, and each of your wills would contain identical provisions, so that the accident of who died first would not determine who got your property. A typical provision might read:

> If my wife fails to survive me, and if all my children predecease me, leaving no issue surviving me, I give 50% of the value of my estate to my heirs at law and 50% of the value of my estate to those persons who would have been my wife's heirs at law had she died at the time of my death.

Another possibility, of course, is to make an alternative gift to your favorite charitable organization.

n. SURVIVORSHIP

If a person to whom you leave property in your will fails to survive you by 120 hours (five days) or more, or if it is impossible to tell who died first (e.g., in an automobile accident), you are deemed to have survived that person and the gift to that person either lapses or goes to the next person in line.

You can provide for a substantially longer period of time than five days. However, if you set too long a period of time, then you delay commencement of probate proceedings because there is no way to determine who the beneficiaries of your will are until such period has elapsed. A 30-day survivorship clause is a reasonable compromise.

Such a provision might read as follows:

> No person named in my will shall be deemed to have survived me unless living on the thirtieth (30th) day after my death.

In a large estate, the presumption of survivorship in case of simultaneous deaths may be reversed for death tax purposes. Such a clause might state that if you and your spouse die simultaneously, your spouse will be deemed to have survived you.

o. GUARDIAN

If you have children who are minors (any unmarried child under the age of 18), then you should provide in your will for the appointment of a guardian in case both you and your spouse die while one or more of your children is a minor.

The function of a guardian is to take the place of a deceased parent in caring for the minor, including facilitating the minor's educational, social, and other activities, authorizing medical or other professional care, and other matters relating to the minor's physical and mental well-being.

A guardian is appointed by the court as part of formal guardianship proceedings, and the court is required to appoint the person most suitable for taking care of the minor. A request that a certain person be appointed guardian of your minor children must be taken into account by the court, but the court is not bound by your designation. However, unless the person you choose as guardian is unsuitable to take care of your children, the court will appoint that person.

The will is a good place to put your designation or selection of guardian. However, this is not the only place that you can indicate your selection. It would be sufficient if you wrote a letter, left an affidavit, or stated in some other written document whom you wished the court to appoint as the guardian.

If the natural parents of a minor are not living together, and the parent having custody of the minor dies, the surviving parent has a legal right to custody of the minor unless there exists some compelling reason for placing the minor in the custody of someone else. The "best-interest-of-the-child" standard, which a court applies in a custody dispute between two parents, say, during a divorce proceeding, does not apply to custody disputes between a natural parent and another person. A natural parent will be denied custody only if unfit, that is, unwilling or unable to care for the child, or, if the parent is fit, if giving custody to the child would be detrimental to the child. Even in the rare case where the surviving parent is denied custody, that parent would be entitled to reasonable visitation privileges with the child.

In one of the few cases in Oregon in which the noncustodial parent was denied custody, the court left custody of a 15-year-old child with a nonrelative who had raised the child since two months of age. The court found that the parent was a virtual stranger to the child. In another case the court refused to grant custody of minor children to a mother where the children disliked the mother and refused to live with her.

Therefore, if you are a parent with custody of a minor child, and the other natural parent is still alive, your designation of another guardian will normally not be effective. However, you may still designate a guardian other than the child's other natural parent in case the other parent does not want custody or dies before you do, or, in rare cases, if a court were to find that the other natural parent was unfit.

10
SIMULTANEOUS DEATHS, SLAYERS, AND DISCLAIMERS

Survivorship is a critical factor in determining who gets your property at your death. As a general rule, if a devisee under your will, the beneficiary of your life insurance policy, or the other co-owner of your joint and survivorship property survives you, that person gets the property. If that person does not survive you, he or she does not get the property.

Oregon has special laws to fill the gaps and to vary this usual rule of survivorship in certain situations.

a. SIMULTANEOUS DEATHS

The basic rule is that where two persons die simultaneously, such as in a common accident, the property of each person will be distributed as if that person has survived the other one. If the right of a beneficiary to receive certain property is conditioned on surviving someone else, and both people die simultaneously, then the beneficiary will be deemed to have died first. For instance, suppose you give some property in your will to a favorite nephew and you both die in the same car accident. The property will be distributed as if the nephew had died first.

If two people owning property in a form of joint and survivorship ownership die simultaneously, half the property will be distributed as if one had survived and half as if the other had survived. In a recent Oregon case, for example, a husband and wife died in a common boat accident. They had owned all their property jointly with right of survivorship, and neither had left a will. One half of the property went to the wife's heirs, who were a son and daughter by a prior marriage, and the other half went to the husband's heirs, who were three sisters and a brother.

If the insured and the beneficiary under a life or accident insurance policy die simultaneously, the policy proceeds will be distributed as if the insured had survived the beneficiary, which means that the proceeds will go to any named contingent beneficiary, if living, otherwise to the insured's probate estate.

These rules apply only when there is insufficient evidence that the persons died other than simultaneously. In most situations, if it is established that one outlived the other even by a minute, then the person living the extra minute will be the survivor, the survivor's estate will get the property, and there is no simultaneous death.

This is not the case, however, with probate property. A special statute requires that for an heir (if there is no will) or a devisee (if there is a will) to take a share of probate property, the heir or devisee must survive the decedent by at least 120 hours (five days). This does not conflict with the simultaneous death rule. Take the earlier example of the gift in your will to your favorite nephew. If you and he die simultaneously, he does not get his share; if he dies four days after you do, he does not get his share.

These rules do not apply if you provide otherwise in a will or other document. For instance, it is not uncommon in wills to provide that a devisee must survive you by some time longer than five days. A sample and the purpose of such a provision is discussed in chapter 9. There could be agreements among joint tenants or provisions in life insurance policies that similarly alter the usual rule of survivorship.

b. SLAYERS

Another statute deals with the situation in which a person who is to receive property from another person, whether by will, survivorship, or otherwise, kills the other person. The general thrust of the statute is that the person doing the killing, called the slayer, does not get the property. The statute accomplishes this by treating the slayer as if he or she had predeceased the person killed, called the decedent, even though the slayer survives the decedent.

For the law to apply, the slayer must take, or procure the taking of, the life of the decedent "with felonious intent." This can be established either by a conviction of such crimes as murder or manslaughter or by other evidence that such killing was "felonious and intentional." It might be possible, for instance, for a person to be acquitted and found not guilty of murder or manslaughter, but nevertheless be found by the probate court to have feloniously and intentionally killed the decedent. The underlying premise, of course, is that a person should not profit from his or her own wrongdoing.

The application of this law to specific types of property is as follows:

1. Probate property

Any property that the slayer would have received as an heir (if there is no will), or as a devisee (if there is a will), is treated as if the slayer had predeceased the decedent.

2. Joint and survivorship property

The slayer gets an undivided one-half interest in the property for the rest of his or her life. The heirs or devisees of the decedent other than the slayer get the balance of the interest in the property. For example, suppose the decedent and the slayer own rental property together. Under the rule, the slayer will get half of the rental income for the rest of his or her life, but will have no interest in the property at the time of his or her death. If the slayer had survived, but not killed, the decedent, the slayer would have been entitled to all the income for life and could have given it away in a will at the time of his or her death.

3. Life estates and remainders

If the slayer owns a remainder interest and the decedent was the life tenant, the life estate passes on to the decedent's heirs or devisees for a period of time equal to the normal life expectancy of the decedent, after which title will vest solely in the slayer.

4. Life insurance

If the slayer is the primary beneficiary on a policy on the life of the decedent, the proceeds go to the secondary beneficiary or, if there is none, the proceeds are distributed as part of the decedent's estate.

c. DISCLAIMERS

Another law that changes the usual rule of survivorship deals with a person's right not to have property forced on him or her. Although it may seem odd for a person to refuse to accept property that is either left under a will or given as a lifetime gift, there may be several good reasons for doing so.

First, you may discover that because of a change in circumstances, poor planning, or simply a desire not to be involved with a disfavored relative who is also getting an interest in the same property, you would like to disclaim (or, as it is sometimes called, renounce) all your interest in the property. For instance, suppose a grandfather left a house with a life estate to your father, from whom you have been estranged for years, remainder to you. It might be easier for you to disclaim your remainder interest in that property rather than having to deal with taking care of the house with your father.

A second reason might be that you already have a large estate and do not need more property. For instance, suppose a parent left you part of the parent's estate and provided in a will that if you predeceased the parent, your interest would go to your children. You could disclaim your interest, in which event it would go directly from your parent to your children. Such a transfer would not be considered a gift from you to your children for federal gift tax purposes.

Or suppose, as a third reason, that you are having financial problems and are fighting off creditors. If you receive an inheritance, it might be reached by your creditors. By disclaiming your inheritance (and having it possibly go to another close family member), you can prevent your creditors from reaching the inheritance.

If you are entitled to receive property that is subject to disclaimer and die or become incapacitated before you can effect a disclaimer, your personal representative, guardian, or conservator can do it for you. You can disclaim less than all the property to which you are entitled.

The disclaimer must be in writing, must be delivered to the personal representative or other appropriate person, may have to be filed with the probate court, and, if it deals with real property, must be recorded. A disclaimer "relates back" and becomes effective as of the date of death of the decedent or as of some other designated date.

The rules on disclaimers come from two sources: Oregon statute and a federal gift tax statute, which determines whether a disclaimer is qualified and thus escapes gift taxes. Although there are some conflicts between the statutes, the following rules are generally true under both laws.

(a) For an heir or devisee of a present interest in probate property (i.e., some outright gift), the interest must be disclaimed within nine months after the decedent's death. In such a case, the property will be distributed as if the disclaimant (the person disclaiming) had predeceased the decedent. If the interest is a future interest, it must be disclaimed within nine months after the interest becomes vested. The two most common future interests are a remainder following a life estate and an interest in a trust, to come into effect only after another beneficiary of the trust has died. In such cases, the property will be distributed as if the disclaimant had predeceased the life tenant or the income beneficiary of a trust.

(b) Powers of appointment are discussed in chapter 5. The appointee, that is, the person to whom the donee appointed the property in the donee's will, may disclaim the property appointed within nine months of the donee's death. The property will be distributed under the donee's will as if the appointee had predeceased the donee of the power.

(c) A beneficiary may disclaim all interest in the proceeds of an insurance policy within nine months of the insured's death. In that case, the beneficiary will be deemed to have predeceased the insured, and the proceeds will go to any living contingent beneficiary or to the insured's probate estate.

(d) A joint owner can disclaim an interest in joint and survivorship property, but generally it must be done within nine months after the property is put into joint ownership. In such a case, the disclaiming joint owner will be deemed to have predeceased the joint owner setting up the property.

(e) A disclaimer cannot be made if the person who intends to disclaim has accepted the property or any of its benefits before making the disclaimer. Examples of acceptance include use of the property or accepting dividends, interest, or rent from the property, directing others to sell or otherwise deal with the property, or receiving payment or other consideration for making the disclaimer.

11
MARRIAGE AND WILLS

a. PROPERTY RIGHTS OF SPOUSES

Many married couples place most or all of their property in joint and survivorship ownership. This is usually done as a matter of convenience and to avoid probate on the death of the first spouse. Other couples keep some or all of their properties in separate ownership. In large estates, separate ownership between spouses will open up estate tax savings possibilities.

1. Divorce

When it comes time to divide up the property in a divorce, the court will settle the property division if the couple cannot work out their own agreement. The law assumes that both spouses have contributed equally to the acquisition of property during the marriage, whether or not it is jointly or separately owned.

In addition to an equitable share of the marital assets, one spouse may be entitled to support or alimony from the other. This support might be temporary or permanent depending on the respective earning abilities and other financial factors of the two spouses.

2. Death

All property owned by the spouses jointly with right of survivorship automatically passes to the surviving spouse. Property in the sole name of a deceased spouse will pass on to the surviving spouse only if the will so provides. If the deceased spouse left no will, the surviving spouse would receive his or her statutory share as heir.

A surviving spouse has the following rights to the probate property of a deceased spouse:

(a) The right to continue to occupy the family home and to receive support during probate

(b) The right to act as personal representative

(c) The right to inherit one-half of the probate property if there is no will and no surviving children of a prior marriage, or all the probate property if there are no issue or issue only of the present marriage

(d) The right to elect against the will and take a share of the probate property. A surviving spouse's elective share is discussed in chapter 15.

A person who was not married to the decedent but who qualifies as a surviving spouse for inheritance only (see chapter 7) is not entitled to elect against the will of the deceased spouse. However, if the deceased spouse did not leave a will, the surviving spouse for inheritance only is entitled to inherit, to act as personal representative, and to continue to occupy the family abode and receive support.

These laws govern probate property only. If the deceased spouse dies without probate property, the surviving spouse will have nothing against which his or her rights can be asserted.

A spouse cannot give away property that is jointly owned and that requires signatures of both spouses. But there is no rule in Oregon that can stop a spouse from giving away his or her probate property during his or her lifetime, even if the intent is to deprive the other spouse of the property at death or dissolution of marriage.

In one case, Walter, who was married to Dorothy, deeded a piece of real property in his own name to his mother and stepfather, so that they each owned an undivided one-third interest as tenants in common. Walter died intestate and his one-third interest passed to Dorothy. Dorothy sued Walter's mother and stepfather claiming that the conveyance was void as an intent by Walter to defeat her rights as wife. The court ruled against Dorothy, holding that the mere fact that Walter intended to deprive her of the property was not sufficient grounds to set aside the conveyance.

b. MARITAL PROPERTY AGREEMENTS

Agreements between spouses can waive the interests granted by law in each other's property either in divorce or at death. They can also grant greater rights to each other than the minimum granted by law. These agreements can be made prior to and in contemplation of marriage or during marriage. Both types of agreements are enforceable provided that they are in writing and entered into validly.

1. Premarital agreements

Premarital agreements, also called prenuptial agreements, are carefully scrutinized by the courts because engaged couples frequently do not know much about each other's property and the agreements are the consequence of emotion rather than logic. They are often challenged at the time of divorce or death of one of the spouses.

Oregon courts have ruled that when parties are engaged to be married, there exists a relationship of trust requiring good faith and full and frank disclosure of all assets. A valid premarital agreement must meet the following conditions:

(a) The parties must sign the agreement voluntarily. It should not be done in haste, but should be done long enough before the wedding to enable both parties to have time to examine and understand the agreement. An agreement would not be voluntary if on the way to the church, one party says to the other, "here, sign this agreement or I won't marry you."

(b) The agreement cannot be unfair to one party unless that party had full disclosure of the other party's property and financial obligations or waived the right to such disclosure. The purpose of this requirement is to avoid overreaching, concealment of assets, or sharp dealing by one party. Each party should attach to the agreement a complete list of property each party owns, with estimated values, and a list of all long-term obligations.

(c) Each party should be represented by his and her own attorney. If one party refuses to retain a separate attorney, the agreement may still be valid, provided the party was offered the opportunity to consult with an attorney and declined to do so, and the agreement is fair and voluntarily entered into.

2. Postnuptial agreements

Postnuptial agreements do not require the same precautions since presumably the spouses are familiar with each other's property. Nevertheless, the same precautions should be followed before signing the agreement.

3. Different kinds of agreements

Marital property agreements can take many forms, but they generally fall into two main categories.

The first kind contemplates that each party will keep his or her assets in separate ownership. Typically, these agreements provide that each party releases all claims against the other's property in case of divorce or death. Each spouse is free to dispose of, manage, or otherwise deal with any separate property including the right to dispose by will. A provision that no alimony be paid will usually be enforced only where each spouse has sufficient assets of his or her own to remain self-supporting.

The second type of agreement assumes that the parties have commingled all their marital assets and own everything in joint and survivorship ownership. The planning is a little more complicated if it is a second marriage and each spouse wants to protect the children of a first marriage. Since all the property is owned jointly, there will be no probate on the first death. Typically the wills provide that upon the second death, half the property goes to the children of the spouse first to die, and half goes to the children of the spouse second to die. To protect the children of the spouse first to die, such an agreement must have the following provisions:

(a) Each spouse agrees to sign a will containing agreed upon terms.

(b) During the joint lives of the spouses, both agree to neither amend nor revoke their wills without the consent of the other.

(c) After the death of the spouse first to die, the will of the surviving spouse will become irrevocable.

(d) If for any reason the survivor's will is revoked (e.g., upon the remarriage of the surviving spouse), the surviving spouse will sign a new will containing terms consistent with the agreement.

(e) Each spouse waives his or her claim to an elective share in the other spouse's solely owned property or a claim to support or any other claim that a surviving spouse generally has.

(f) After the death of the spouse first to die, the surviving spouse will not give away or otherwise transfer any assets without adequate consideration. This is to avoid the possibility that after the death of the spouse first to die, the surviving spouse simply gives away all the property and defeats the interests of the children of the deceased spouse.

(g) The contract can also cover the manner in which the spouses use the property during their joint lives, and may deal separately with the manner and treatment of the wife's own property, the husband's own property, and the jointly owned assets, if any.

Although this form of agreement avoids probate on the death of the first spouse, it creates two other problems. The agreement may disqualify the property for the federal estate tax marital deduction on the death of the first spouse. It also severely restricts the freedom and flexibility of the surviving spouse to manage and use the marital property. In effect, the children of the deceased spouse will always be looking over the shoulder of the surviving spouse to make certain that the children's expectancy is not being mismanaged.

An alternative to this arrangement might be to require that when the first spouse dies, the surviving spouse place half of the marital assets in an irrevocable trust for the children of the deceased spouse. The surviving spouse would have the right to income and could even be the trustee. The surviving spouse would be free to deal with the other half of the marital assets as desired.

c. AGREEMENTS FOR UNMARRIED COUPLES

A 1978 court decision established the basis for dealing with the breakup of relationships of unmarried couples. The court established the rule that property is to be distributed on the basis of the express or implied intent of the couple. If there is no written agreement, then the court is required to look at particular circumstances of the couple.

Cohabitation, joint bank accounts, joint purchases, and shared income would all be evidence of an intent to pool resources for common benefit during the relationship. This would warrant an approximately equal division of the assets of the couple, regardless of whose name they were in.

If the court cannot find a general intent to share all the property that the couple accumulated during the relationship, it will review the intent and award each item of property separately. In one case, the court concluded that the couple intended to share the household items equally, but separately maintain large purchases, like the car, home, and motorcycle.

There is a great need for a written agreement between unmarried partners. If the relationship ends, the couple is not usually in agreement about the division of property. Unlike the dissolution of a marriage, there are no rules requiring an equitable division of property. There are also no rules regarding alimony or other maintenance payments.

Absence of a written agreement creates even more of a problem for unmarried couples upon the death of one of the parties, particularly if the deceased party owned all or most of the property accumulated during the relationship in his or her own name and failed to make a will leaving such property to the surviving party. In this situation, the survivor will get nothing, unless the deceased party did not leave a will and the survivor qualifies as a surviving spouse for inheritance.

d. ARE YOU REALLY MARRIED?

In view of the stark difference between the legal rights and duties of married and unmarried couples, it should not be too surprising that disputes arise over whether a couple is lawfully married, particularly after one or both of them have died.

Oregon requires a *ceremonial* marriage and does not recognize a so-called *common-law* marriage. Common-law marriages are recognized in some states, such as Idaho. Typically, such states require that the couple agree to be husband and wife, hold themselves out as husband and wife, and cohabit and otherwise mutually assume the marital rights, duties, and obligations. No ceremony is required to validate a common-law marriage in those states that recognize it.

For a marriage made in Oregon to be valid, it must be solemnized. The couple must first obtain medical certificates signed by a licensed physician and a marriage license issued by a county clerk. Then they must have their marriage solemnized by assenting or declaring in the presence of a minister, county clerk, or judicial officer, and at least two witnesses that they take each other to be husband and wife.

While Oregon law does not recognize a common-law marriage entered into in Oregon, it will recognize common-law marriages validly consummated in states that do recognize them.

Oregon recognizes an unmarried survivor of a deceased person as that person's surviving spouse and heir for inheritance purposes only, if the unmarried survivor meets certain qualifications (see chapter 7). However, unlike a common-law marriage, the two persons are not treated as married for any other purpose.

12
GIFTS TO MINORS

If you want to make a gift to a minor, you should take certain precautionary steps to prevent misuse. Gifts can be made during your lifetime, or at your death by a provision in your will or living trust.

a. WHAT IS A MINOR?

In Oregon, a minor is any person who is NOT —

    (a) 18 years of age or older

    (b) married and 17 years of age or older

    (c) 16 years of age or older and emancipated (This requires a special court hearing where the court concludes that the minor is mature enough to manage his or her own affairs without parental assistance.

b. MINORS AND THE LAW

The law protects minors in two ways. First, the law says a minor can avoid transactions entered into while a minor. Second, the law provides that certain persons will have authority to manage a minor's affairs.

If you make a gift to a minor, it will be difficult for anyone to purchase the property or otherwise contract with the minor. A minor may disaffirm any acquisition or sale of property or any contract made while a minor, either during minority or within a reasonable time after reaching majority.

This rule protects the minor, but it also makes it difficult for the minor to deal with property. If the property requires management, the court would appoint an adult or a bank to manage it during the beneficiary's minority.

c. CUSTODIANSHIPS

One of the best ways to make a small gift to a minor is through a custodianship. Under Oregon's law on gifts to minors, the Uniform Transfers to Minors Act, you can use a custodianship for present or future gifts of any kind of property, real or personal.

1. How to set up a custodianship

You can establish a custodianship either by lifetime transfer or by naming a custodian to receive property that is to be transferred to a minor at some future date, such as under a will or as a beneficiary of a life insurance policy. A lifetime transfer to a custodian is irrevocable and conveys to and vests title and ownership of the property in the minor. In effect, the custodian holds and manages the minor's property for the minor until the minor reaches majority and receives possession of the property.

To establish a custodianship, you need to use this phrase: "as custodian for (name of minor) under the Oregon Uniform Transfers to Minors Act." By using this simple phrase, you set up and adopt a statutory structure, similar to a detailed trust agreement, for managing and protecting a minor's property.

2. Who can be a custodian?

Any adult, including the transferor, can be a custodian. The custodian can be, but need not be, a parent or other relative of the minor. A financial institution with trust powers can be a custodian, but will seldom be a practical choice. Custodianships should generally be used for relatively small gifts (whatever amount you are willing to turn over to the minor at age 21) and most financial institutions will not act as a custodian if the value of the property is less than $100,000.

If federal estate taxes are a concern for the transferor (generally, if the estate is more than $600,000 — see chapter 17), the transferor should not act as custodian. If the transferor acts as custodian and then dies before the minor is 21 and receives the property, the value of the property will be included in the transferor's estate for estate tax purposes.

3. Duties and powers of the custodian

A custodian may deliver or pay to the minor or expend for the minor's benefit as much of the custodial property as he or she considers advisable for the minor's use and benefit, or the custodian may accumulate the income and wait to distribute all the income and principal to the minor at majority. In exercising this discretion, the custodian may disregard the duty or ability of a parent to support the child or the fact that there may be other income or property available to the minor.

A custodian has the duty to do the following:

(a) Take control, collect, hold, manage, invest, and reinvest the property

(b) Keep the property separate from all other property

(c) Keep records of all transactions, including information necessary for the preparation of the minor's tax returns. A custodian has all the powers necessary to carry out these duties.

4. Court supervision

No court regularly monitors a custodianship. On rare occasions, court intervention may occur if the minor, or someone on the minor's behalf, petitions the court because —

(a) the custodian fails to use the custodial property for the minor's benefit,

(b) the custodian should be removed for cause or required to file a bond, or

(c) the minor wants an accounting.

5. Expenses and compensation

The costs of a custodianship should be nominal. It can be set up with little or no help from an attorney, and there are no court costs or bond premiums. A custodian is entitled to reimbursement for reasonable expenses and, if the custodian is a person other than the transferor, reasonable compensation.

6. Ending the custodianship

A custodianship ends and the custodian must turn over the property when the minor reaches age 21 (even though a minor reaches majority at age 18 for most other purposes). If the minor dies before age 21, the custodian must transfer the property to the minor's estate, which will go to the minor's parents in most cases.

In two cases the custodian must transfer the property to the minor at age 18. First, if you leave property to a minor in a will or trust and do not provide for a custodianship, a personal representative, trustee, or conservator can transfer property worth up to $10,000 (or move if a court approves) to a custodian. Second, if someone owes a minor money or holds property of a minor worth up to $5,000, that person can transfer the money or property to a minor. In either case, the minor gets the property at age 18.

7. Income taxes

Because custodial property belongs to the minor, any income earned from the property is taxed to the minor, regardless of whether the custodian spends it for the minor or accumulates it. If, however, income is used to satisfy a parent's obligation of support (e.g., if the custodian buys food or clothing for the minor), then the income will be taxed to the parent. Under the 1986 Tax Reform Act, if unearned income of a minor under the age of 14, including income earned on custodial property, exceeds $1,000, the excess will be taxed at the highest marginal tax rate of the minor's parents.

d. CONSERVATORSHIPS

A conservatorship is a court-supervised procedure for managing and protecting the property of either a minor or an incapacitated adult. (See chapter 13 for conservatorships for adults.) A conservator is the person or financial institution appointed by the court to handle the minor's property.

A conservatorship must be distinguished from a guardianship, which is the procedure for determining custody and ensuring the proper care of a minor. However, the same person can be both guardian and conservator.

1. How to set up a conservatorship

A conservatorship is established by court order upon petition by an interested party. The court must determine that the minor owns money or property that requires management or protection. It would be unusual to make a lifetime gift to a minor with the intent that a conservator be appointed to manage the property.

A petition must be filed with a probate court naming the minor and the proposed conservator and giving information about the minor's property and family. A notice of petition must be given to the minor if the minor is 14 years of age or older, to the minor's parents, guardian, or custodian, and to other interested persons.

If no objections are filed, then the court appoints the conservator and sets the amount of the bond. The conservator must file an inventory of the property within 90 days of appointment.

2. Who can be a conservator?

Any financial institution with trust powers and any individual who is not incapacitated, financially incapable, a minor, or the minor's health care provider may act as a conservator. Two or more individuals may act as co-conservators.

The court will appoint the most suitable person who is willing to serve after giving consideration to the specific circumstances of the minor, any stated desire by the minor, any preference expressed by a parent of the minor, the minor's estate or property, and any impact on ease of administration that may result from the appointment.

3. Duties and powers of a conservator

A conservator must use the minor's property for the minor's care, support, education, or benefit. In determining standards for such payments, the conservator may consider the recommendations of the minor's parents or guardian unless the conservator knows that the parent or guardian is deriving personal financial benefit from such payments, including relief from any personal duty to support.

This is different from the duty of a custodian, who may ignore any duty of support in making payments for a minor. A conservator must also consider the size of the estate, the minor's accustomed standard of living, and other funds or sources available for the minor's support. Again, this is different from the duty of a custodian, who may ignore other funds available to the minor.

A conservator generally has all the powers necessary to manage the minor's property and to carry out the conservator's duties. He or she has all the powers of a trustee and of a guardian for the minor if none has been appointed.

4. Court supervision

A conservator must file an accounting with the court each year within 30 days of the anniversary of the conservator's appointment. He or she must also provide a copy of the accounting to the guardian and to the minor (if the minor is 14 years or older and capable of understanding it). The accounting must contain a list of all receipts and disbursements made during the year, a summary of any purchases or sales of property, and any other significant events that occurred during the year concerning the minor's financial affairs.

A conservator must also file a surety bond equal to the value of the minor's property plus one year's income. It may be for a lower amount if the court orders that certain property is to be frozen, or if the court bars the conservator from selling.

A conservator has the same liabilities and duties as a trustee and is subject to the same penalties for breach of those duties.

5. Expenses

There can be substantial costs in setting up and managing a conservatorship. The services of an attorney are required to establish the conservatorship, to prepare the inventory and annual accounting, and to advise the conservator on various matters. Court costs and bond premiums must also be paid. A conservator is entitled to reasonable compensation and expenses. These are to be paid out of the minor's property.

6. Ending a conservatorship

A conservatorship is terminated either when the minor becomes an adult or upon the minor's death, whichever comes first. A minor is defined in the conservatorship statute as any person who has not attained 18 years of age.

A conservatorship may be terminated early if the property consists solely of personal property worth less than $10,000. In that case, it would be distributed to some responsible adult for the minor's benefit.

7. Incapacity

If a minor is incapable of handling his or her own affairs when the age of majority is attained, then the conservatorship may be continued for the period of the incapacity. The incapacity must be established to the court's satisfaction.

8. Multiple conservatorships

If two or more minors are children of a common parent, their conservatorships may be consolidated into one. Each minor's assets, however, would be segregated and separately managed.

e. TRUSTS

Trusts have the advantage of being flexible enough that you can tailor them precisely to your particular concerns or goals. For example, you can set up an irrevocable living trust for a minor to provide for the minor's education with less income tax costs to you.

1. How to set up a trust for a minor

A trust is a contract between you and the trustees. A living trust is drafted and signed by you and the trustee, after which you fund the trust by transferring title to certain property. A testamentary trust is set out for your will and funded after your death when your personal representative transfers the property to the trustee.

2. Who can be a trustee?

Any individual or financial institution with trust powers can act as trustee. There are no requirements that an individual must meet to qualify, except those that you might set out in the trust document.

3. Duties and powers

The primary duty of the trustee is to carry out the wishes set out in your trust document. For example, you can direct the trustee to make distributions of income to the minor for support only.

Under the Uniform Trustees' Powers Act, which is automatically part of your trust unless you direct otherwise, a trustee has all the powers necessary to carry out the duties, including power to invest and reinvest in accordance with the "prudent man" rule. However, you can limit the trustee's powers by specifying what kinds of investments the trustee can make.

4. Court supervision

A trustee must provide an annual accounting to the minor on request. There is no court supervision unless the minor or someone on the minor's behalf petitions the court to review the trustee's action. The trustee is required to post a bond only if the trust document requires it.

5. Expenses

Normally, the trust document provides for reasonable compensation and expenses for the trustee. However, you may set out a specific compensation formula. The other major costs are attorney's fees for setting up the trust and any advice the attorney may provide.

6. Ending a trust

The termination of a trust is up to you. For example, if you are setting up a trust to fund a college education, you will want it to extend until the minor is at least 22. If the property is of substantial value, you may want to extend it even longer.

7. Incapacity

You can provide that if the beneficiary is incapacitated at the scheduled age for distribution, the trustee can continue the trust so long as such incapacity continues, including, if necessary, for the rest of the minor's life.

8. Multiple trusts or beneficiaries

You may direct that a single trust be set up for more than one minor. This is called a "spray" or "sprinkling" trust because the trustee is authorized to spray or sprinkle funds among the beneficiaries based on their separate medical, educational, or other needs. If one beneficiary has greater needs than another, then that beneficiary will receive greater benefits from the trust. There is no duty in such a trust to treat each beneficiary equally. This is a good plan when you are not certain that the property in the trust will be sufficient to meet the needs of each beneficiary if there is equal distribution.

f. GUARDIANSHIPS

Chapter 9 discussed the importance of naming a guardian in your will for your minor children. This section describes the guardianship procedure in more detail.

1. Setting up a guardianship

A guardianship is established in the same way as a conservatorship, and frequently even the same person may be appointed guardian and conservator.

A guardian is required to file a report with the court annually, within 30 days after each anniversary of appointment. In the report the guardian must give information about the minor, such as where the minor lives, the minor's physical and mental condition, and the guardian's activities during the year in taking care of the minor.

2. Who can be a guardian?

Only an individual may be appointed guardian and that person must have the same qualifications as a conservator. A financial institution cannot act as a guardian.

3. Duties of a guardian

A guardian has the powers and responsibilities of a parent who has the legal custody of a child, except that the guardian has no obligation to support the minor beyond the support that the minor receives from other sources. The guardian is not liable for the acts of the minor. The guardian may consent to the marriage or adoption of the minor.

A guardian may receive money and personal property deliverable to the minor and apply money and property for the support, care, and education of the minor. The guardian must conserve any excess funds for the minor's needs. A guardian may not use the minor's funds for room and board furnished by the guardian or by the guardian's spouse, parent, or child without prior court approval.

g. REVOCABLE TRUST ACCOUNTS AND OTHER POD ACCOUNTS FOR MINORS

You can open up a bank account in your own name as trustee for a minor. Such arrangements are simple to set up, but are not necessarily good ways to make gifts to minors.

Since you are treated as the owner of the account until your death, all this arrangement will do is avoid probate of that account. Unless you have also put all your other property into nonprobate ownership, you will not avoid probate except with that account.

One possible advantage is that it does enable immediate distribution to the beneficiary upon the death of the trustee. However, these accounts frequently distort estate plans. For instance, if you want to give all your estate in equal shares to your children, but have one trust account for one child, then that child is going to get what is in the trust account plus whatever you give that child under your will.

Financial institution employees are sometimes too casual in the way that they set up such accounts. Sometimes there are signature cards that set out your rights as trustee and when the minor is to get the property. Other times, however, the account will simply state your name as trustee for the minor without any indication as to what happens at your death.

A typical bank card provides for a successor trustee if you die before the minor turns 18. However, if the successor trustee also dies before the minor reaches age 18, then it will be up to the bank to select a trustee. This leaves too much discretion in the management of your financial affairs to the bank.

If the minor dies before you do, then the funds come back into your estate as part of your probate property. If the minor dies before the successor trustee, then all the funds belong to the successor trustee.

There is no provision for the successor trustee's duties and powers, or for what happens if the minor is disabled at the age of 18, or has other problems.

When you die, if a successor trustee must act, then he or she can treat those funds as if they belong absolutely to him or her and not to the beneficiary, unless there is contrary language in the bank signature card.

In short, revocable trust accounts for minors should be used with great caution, only for small amounts of money, and then only after careful review and understanding of the bank signature card.

You should also be cautious about naming minors as beneficiaries of POD accounts with financial institutions, and as TOD beneficiaries on stocks, bonds, and other securities.

If you decide to name a minor as beneficiary of a trust or POD account at a bank or a TOD beneficiary of a security, then provide that if the minor is under 21 at your death, the beneficiary will be a custodian for the minor, under the Oregon Uniform Transfer to Minors Act.

13
PLANNING FOR INCAPACITY

a. HEALTH CARE DECISIONS

In thinking about the possibility that you may become incapable of making decisions for yourself, whether because of illness, accident, or other reasons, you need to plan at two different levels. First, you need to decide who will make health care decisions for you and how those decisions will be made. Second, you should decide how and by whom your property and financial affairs will be managed.

b. NEW HEALTH CARE FORMS

Oregon has two new health care forms — the advance directive and the declaration for mental health treatment. Both forms became available in November 1993.

The advance directive is a form by which you can name representatives to make health care decisions for you if you become incapable of making them yourself. You can also direct how health care decisions will be made for you. It replaces and combines the power of attorney for health care and the directive to physicians. See Sample #3.

The declaration for mental health treatment is a form of more limited scope. You can authorize certain types of mental health treatment if you have a mental health crisis. A sample is not included in this book.

Both new forms are available at hospitals, doctor's offices, through various health care and mental health organizations, and from attorneys. They can also be purchased at stores that sell legal forms.

1. **The advance directive**

The advance directive has two main parts: Part B, in which you can name one or two persons to make health care decisions for you, and Part C, in which you can give instructions on how health care decisions will be made for you. You may fill out Part B, Part C, or both. For instance, you may have any persons you want to name as your health care representative, but may want to direct your health care providers on how decisions will be made for you in case of your incapacity. In such cases, you would fill out Part C, but not Part B.

In Part C you can state whether or not you want tube feeding or other kinds of life support, such as a respirator, if you have any one of four critical conditions. These provisions would apply if you are close to death or terminally ill; you are permanently unconscious or in a persistent vegetative state; you have an advanced progressive illness, such as Alzheimer's Disease; or life support would cause extraordinary suffering.

You can also insert additional conditions or instructions in Part C. For instance, if you have a degenerative disease and know that there are certain treatments you would want and certain treatments you would not want if the disease got worse, you could state those instructions in this part. You can also direct that you want to be an anatomical donor after your death.

2. **Signing the advance directive**

You must use the specific form set out by law. It contains the required language. The form must be limited to health care decisions and cannot contain instructions on how to manage your property and financial affairs in case you become incapacitated.

You must sign the form in the presence of two witnesses. If you complete both Part B and Part C, then you must sign the form twice, once at the end of Part B and a second time at the end of Part C. The witnesses must sign Part D. They must meet certain qualifications, which are listed at the end of Part D.

SAMPLE #3
THE ADVANCE DIRECTIVE

ADVANCE DIRECTIVE
YOU DO NOT HAVE TO FILL OUT AND SIGN THIS FORM
PART A: IMPORTANT INFORMATION ABOUT THIS ADVANCE DIRECTIVE

This is an important legal document. It can control critical decisions about your health care. Before signing, consider these important facts:

Facts About Part B (Appointing a Health Care Representative)

You have the right to name a person to direct your health care when you cannot do so. This person is called your "health care representative." You can do this by using Part B of this form. Your representative must accept on Part E of this form.

You can write in this document any restrictions you want on how your representative will make decisions for you. Your representative must follow your desires as stated in this document or otherwise made known. If your desires are unknown, your representative must try to act in your best interest. Your representative can resign at any time.

Facts About Part C (Giving Health Care Instructions)

You also have the right to give instructions for health care providers to follow if you become unable to direct your care. You can do this by using Part C of this form.

Facts About Completing This Form

This form is valid only if you sign it voluntarily and when you are of sound mind. If you do not want an advance directive, you do not have to sign this form.

Unless you have limited the duration of this advance directive, it will not expire. If you have set an expiration date, and you become unable to direct your health care before that date, this advance directive will not expire until you are able to make those decisions again.

You may revoke this document at any time. To do so, notify your representative and your health care provider of the revocation.

Despite this document, you have the right to decide your own health care as long as you are able to do so.

If there is anything in this document that you do not understand, ask a lawyer to explain it to you.

You may sign PART B, PART C, or both parts. You may cross out words that do not express your wishes or add words that better express your wishes. Witnesses must sign PART D.

Print your NAME, BIRTHDATE AND ADDRESS here:

_____
(Name)
_____
(Birthdate)
_____
(Address)

Unless revoked or suspended, this advance directive will continue for:

INITIAL ONE:

_____ My entire life
_____ Other period (_____ Years)

Page 1 - OREGON ADVANCE DIRECTIVE

SAMPLE #3 — Continued

PART B: APPOINTMENT OF HEALTH CARE REPRESENTATIVE

I appoint _____ as my health care representative. My representative's address is _____ and telephone number is ( ) _____.

I appoint _____ as my alternate health care representative. My alternate's address and telephone number is ( ) _____.

I authorize my representative (or alternate) to direct my health care when I cannot do so.

NOTE: You may not appoint your doctor, an employee of your doctor, or an owner, operator or employee of your health care facility, unless that person is related to you by blood, marriage or adoption or that person was appointed before your admission into the health care facility.

1. **Limits.** Special Conditions or Instructions: _____

INITIAL IF THIS APPLIES:
_____ I have executed a Health Care Instruction or Directive to Physicians. My representative is to honor it.

2. **Life Support.** "Life support" refers to any medical means for maintaining life, including procedures, devices and medications. If you refuse life support, you will still get routine measures to keep you clean and comfortable.

INITIAL IF THIS APPLIES:
_____ My representative MAY decide about life support for me. (If you do not initial this space, then your representative MAY NOT decide about life support.)

3. **Tube Feeding.** One sort of life support is food and water supplied artificially by medical device, known as tube feeding.

INITIAL IF THIS APPLIES:
_____ My representative MAY decide about tube feeding for me. (If you do not initial this space, then your representative MAY NOT decide about tube feeding.)

_____
(Date)

SIGN HERE TO APPOINT A HEALTH CARE REPRESENTATIVE

_____
(Signature of person making appointment)

PART C: HEALTH CARE INSTRUCTIONS

NOTE: In filling out these instructions, keep the following in mind:
- The term "as my physician recommends" means that you want your physician to try life support if your physician believes it could be helpful and then discontinue it if it is not helping your health condition or symptoms.
- "Life support" and "tube feeding" are defined in Part B above.
- If you refuse tube feeding, you should understand that malnutrition, dehydration and death will probably result.
- You will get care for your comfort and cleanliness, no matter what choices you make.
- You may either give specific instructions by filling out Items 1 to 4 below, or you may use the general instruction provided by Item 5.

Page 2 - OREGON ADVANCE DIRECTIVE

SAMPLE #3 — Continued

Here are my desires about my health care if my doctor and another knowledgeable doctor confirm that I am in a medical condition described below:

1. **Close to Death.** If I am close to death and life support would only postpone the moment of my death:
A. INITIAL ONE:
____ I want to receive tube feeding.
____ I want tube feeding only as my physician recommends.
____ I DO NOT WANT tube feeding.

B. INITIAL ONE:
____ I want any other life support that may apply.
____ I want life support only as my physician recommends.
____ I want NO life support.

2. **Permanently Unconscious.** If I am unconscious and it is very unlikely that I will ever become conscious again:
A. INITIAL ONE:
____ I want to receive tube feeding.
____ I want tube feeding only as my physician recommends.
____ I DO NOT WANT tube feeding.

B. INITIAL ONE:
____ I want any other life support that may apply.
____ I want life support only as my physician recommends.
____ I want NO life support.

3. **Advanced Progressive Illness.** If I have a progressive illness that will be fatal and is in an advanced stage, and I am consistently and permanently unable to communicate by any means, swallow food and water safely, care for myself and recognize my family and other people, and it is very unlikely that my condition will substantially improve:
A. INITIAL ONE:
____ I want to receive tube feeding.
____ I want tube feeding only as my physician recommends.
____ I DO NOT WANT tube feeding.

B. INITIAL ONE:
____ I want any other life support that may apply.
____ I want life support only as my physician recommends.
____ I want NO life support.

4. **Extraordinary Suffering.** If life support would not help my medical condition and would make me suffer permanent and severe pain:
A. INITIAL ONE:
____ I want to receive tube feeding.
____ I want tube feeding only as my physician recommends.
____ I DO NOT WANT tube feeding.

B. INITIAL ONE:
____ I want any other life support that may apply.
____ I want life support only as my physician recommends.
____ I want NO life support.

5. **General Instruction.**
INITIAL IF THIS APPLIES:
____ I do not want my life to be prolonged by life support. I also do not want tube feeding as life support. I want my doctors to allow me to die naturally if my doctor and another knowledgeable doctor confirm I am in any of the medical conditions listed in Items 1 to 4 above.

6. **Additional Conditions or Instructions.** _____
_____
(Insert description of what you want done.)

7. **Other Documents.** A "health care power of attorney" is any document you may have signed to appoint a representative to make health care decisions for you.
INITIAL ONE:
____ I have previously signed a health care power of attorney. I want it to remain in effect unless I appointed a health care representative after signing the health care power of attorney.
____ I have a health care power of attorney, and I REVOKE IT.
____ I DO NOT have a health care power of attorney.

_____
(Date)
SIGN HERE TO GIVE INSTRUCTIONS

_____
(Signature)

Page 3 - OREGON ADVANCE DIRECTIVE

SAMPLE #3 — Continued

PART D: DECLARATION OF WITNESSES

We declare that the person signing this advance directive:

(a) Is personally known to us or has provided proof of identity;
(b) Signed or acknowledged that person's signature on this advance directive in our presence;
(c) Appears to be of sound mind and not under duress, fraud or undue influence;
(d) Has not appointed either of us as health care representative or alternative representative; and
(e) Is not a patient for whom either of us is attending physician.

Witnessed By:

_____   _____
(Signature of Witness/Date)   (Printed Name of Witness)

_____   _____
(Signature of Witness/Date)   (Printed Name of Witness)

NOTE: One witness must not be a relative (by blood, marriage or adoption) of the person signing this advance directive. That witness must also not be entitled to any portion of the person's estate upon death. That witness must also not own, operate or be employed at a health care facility where the person is a patient or resident.

PART E: ACCEPTANCE BY HEALTH CARE REPRESENTATIVE

I accept this appointment and agree to serve as health care representative. I understand I must act consistently with the desire of the person I represent, as expressed in this advance directive or otherwise made known to me. If I do not know the desire of the person I represent, I have a duty to act in what I believe in good faith to be that person's best interest. I understand that this document allows me to decide about that person's health care only while that person cannot do so. I understand that the person who appointed me may revoke this appointment. If I learn that this document has been suspended or revoked, will inform the person's current health care provider if known to me.

_____   _____
(Signature of Health Care Representative)   (Date)

_____
(Printed name)

_____   _____
(Signature of Alternate Health Care Representative) (Date)

_____
(Printed name)

Page 4 - OREGON ADVANCE DIRECTIVE

If you appoint health care representatives, their appointment is not effective unless they date and sign the form in Part E. You should have them sign after you have signed the form. They need not be present when you sign, nor do they need to sign in the presence of your witnesses.

3. Distributing the advance directive

Once your advance directive is signed by you, your witnesses, and your representatives, you should make enough copies to give one copy each to your health care representatives, to your physician or physicians, and to any hospital where you have been a recent patient.

Your physicians and hospital are required to place and keep your advance directive in your medical records. You may also wish to give copies of the directives to family members or close friends who are not named as your representative, and to your attorney and clergy. You should keep the original directive.

4. Making decisions for you

Your health care representative cannot act for you until and unless you become incapable of making your own health care decisions. Your attending physician or a court must determine your incapacity. If you put specific conditions or instructions in the advance directive, then your representative must follow your directions. If you do not, then your representative must act in your best interest. If you do not name a health care representative, then your health care provider must follow your instructions.

5. Former health care documents

The power of attorney for health care and the directive to physicians described in chapter 12 of the last edition continue to be valid in Oregon. If you have signed either form, you may continue to rely on the form as an enforceable expression of your wishes concerning who will make health decisions for you and how they will be made if you become incapacitated.

However, health care professionals recommend that you sign the new advance directive, even if you have already signed the older forms. The new form is more flexible and comprehensive than the older forms and gives you the opportunity to express your wishes in a broader range of health care situations.

Although the directive to physicians is effective for your life, the power of attorney for health care has a term of seven years, and you have to renew it after that time if you want it to continue to be in effect. If you sign the new advance directive, you can make it effective for the rest of your life.

6. Mental health declaration

The declaration for mental health treatment is a new form, available in Oregon for the first time, and does not replace any existing form. It enables you to give advance directions on how you want certain mental health decisions to be made for you if you are incapable of making them yourself. It deals with three types of mental health treatments: convulsive treatment, use of psychoactive medications, and up to 17 days of in-patient care. You cannot authorize these kinds of mental health treatments in an advance directive. This new document is designed primarily for persons with mental health disorders.

c. PROPERTY AND FINANCIAL DECISIONS

There are several tools for handling your property and financial affairs if you become incapacitated. Making sure these tools are in effect while you are still competent can minimize risk of loss of your property and disruption of your business and financial affairs if you become incapacitated.

1. Conservatorships and guardianships

Conservatorships and guardianships for adults are court supervised proceedings for managing and protecting the property and financial affairs and for providing for the care of an adult if needed. At a minimum, you should indicate in writing who your choice would be for guardian or conservator if you become incapacitated. This should be someone you can trust with your financial affairs (for a conservator) and with decisions concerning where you live and what medical care you receive (for a guardian).

A conservatorship ensures maximum protection because of the bond, annual accounts, and court supervision requirements. However, it is also the most costly. A conservatorship terminates at death and cannot, therefore, be used to avoid probate.

A conservatorship will make your financial affairs a matter of public record. It is the only choice for a person needing protection if no advance planning has been done.

2. Power of attorney

A power of attorney is a document that you sign authorizing someone else to act as your agent. You are called the "principal" and the person you appoint is called the "agent" or "attorney-in-fact."

A power of attorney may be either general or limited. A general power of attorney authorizes your agent to sign your name and deal with your property to the same extent that you may. It is a blanket authority given to the agent to act on your behalf with respect to your property. General powers of attorney should be used with great caution.

A limited power of attorney limits the authority to act on certain transactions. For example, you might authorize your stock broker to buy and sell securities for you.

A power of attorney can be used as a planning tool for incapacity because of the special law that authorizes your agent to act if you become disabled or incompetent. (This is called a "durable power of attorney.") A power of attorney is automatically revoked by your death. It also may be revoked by a written document while you are alive. You must be mentally competent to make or revoke a power of attorney. If you do become incompetent after signing a power of attorney, the agent becomes accountable to your conservator for all actions.

The major attraction of a power of attorney is the ease with which it may be signed. Forms are readily available at office supply stores. However, because a power of attorney is so easy to sign and use, it can also be misused. If you want to sign a power of attorney to plan for your possible incapacity, you should do so with the assistance of an attorney.

3. Revocable living trust

Chapters 5 and 6 described the funded revocable living trust. If you are considering this as a means of planning for incapacity, consider the following:

(a) This kind of trust is expensive to set up.

(b) The trust agreement can be tailored to your particular desires and needs regarding the management and distribution of your assets while you are incapacitated.

(c) A living trust can be used to avoid probate, so your financial affairs do not become public record at your death.

(d) A living trust is generally more effective and reliable than a power of attorney, which may not be accepted by financial institutions, stock brokers, or title companies.

4. Joint bank accounts

If you want to use a joint bank account to plan for incapacity, here are a few suggestions:

(a) Set up the account only with someone you trust. Your spouse of 40 years is a safe choice.

(b) If you want the other person to have power over your account, but you don't want the account to go automatically to that person at your death, you should grant the person a limited power of attorney, but keep the account in your own name. Most banks have forms for this purpose. Use a joint and survivorship bank account only if you also want the person to have the funds in the account at your death.

(c) Sign a letter of understanding with the other joint owner setting out how and when the funds in the account are to be used.

A joint bank account is easy to set up, and for that reason it is easy to abuse. There is always the risk that the other joint owner may predecease you, in which case the account will be back in your own name. If you are already incapacitated, then a conservator may have to be appointed. Another risk is that the other joint owner may have tax, creditor, or domestic problems, in which case you may lose the funds in your joint account, or the account may end up in litigation.

A joint bank account is only a partial solution. You would still have to plan for the management of your other property if you became incapacitated.

d. LONG-TERM HEALTH CARE

A major concern for older persons today is the prospect that an extended stay in a nursing home may deplete their estates and leave them penniless. Special nursing home insurance is now available to cover such costs. In addition, with advance planning, a family can take steps to minimize financial impoverishment and conserve assets when a person must be in a nursing home for a long period. The primary means of conserving assets for a patient in a nursing home is to qualify for Medicaid without having to spend all the patient's assets and thus impoverish the patient first.

Medicaid is a combined federal-state medical assistance program which pays the nursing home costs for persons who are too poor to pay. It also covers other health care services, such as residential care facilities, adult foster care, in home care, physician services, prescription drugs, and medical transportation.

To qualify for Medicaid, you must meet both an income and resource test. To meet the income test, your gross income must be $1,374 or less per month, an amount which periodically changes.

If your income exceeds the gross income limitation, then you face the risk of not being able to qualify for Medicaid yet not being able to afford the cost of a nursing home. One way to qualify is to sign a special form of irrevocable trust known as an "income-cap trust." Basically, you agree with the state that all of your income will be transferred to the trustee, to be distributed according to Medicaid priorities. The trustee will have authority to make distributions from the trust for your personal needs, administrative costs, family support obligations, nursing home, and other health care costs. Any funds remaining in the trust at your death must be turned over to the state.

To meet the resource, or asset, test, you cannot own any "available" resources, other than excluded resources. If you are married, then your spouse's resources are considered available to you, even if the resources are in your spouse's name alone. A resource is considered available to you if you or your spouse have the right to sell or use it. Examples include bank and brokerage accounts, stocks and bonds, cash value life insurance, real property, motor vehicles, and retirement accounts.

The primary excluded resources are the following:

(a) Cash up to $2,000

(b) Your home, provided you are residing in it or reasonably expect to return to it, or if your spouse, a minor or disabled child, or other dependent relative is residing in it

(c) One automobile and all personal and household belongings

(d) Burial merchandise, such as a casket and vault or cemetery plot

(e) A burial fund, prepaid burial insurance, or a life insurance policy of up to $1,500.

If you are married, then the spouse not applying for Medicaid, called the "community spouse," may retain some of your income and resources. The purpose is to prevent the community spouse from becoming impoverished.

Any resources that do not qualify as excluded resources, and, if you are married, any resources not allocated to the community spouse, must be spent or given away before you can qualify for Medicaid.

In order to preserve resources in excess of excluded resources and resources allocated to a community spouse, you have to transfer resources out of your name, typically to children. Giving away resources to qualify for Medicaid, however, requires long-term advance planning because of the ability of the state to look back and penalize you for gifts made too soon before you apply for Medicaid. This rule does not apply to gifts between spouses.

When you apply for Medicaid, the state looks back and analyzes all gifts which you made during the 36 months prior to the date of your application. If you make a gift out of a trust, the look-back period is 60 months. Prior to October 1, 1993, the look-back period was 30 months for both outright gifts and gifts out of trust. Any gifts made before the applicable look-back period do not need to be reported.

If you make any gifts during the look-back period, then you may be ineligible for Medicaid for the number of months equal to the value of all gifts made divided by the average monthly cost of nursing home care in Oregon. In 1995 this average monthly cost was $2,595. Whether or not a gift within the look-back period makes you ineligible for a period of time depends on the value of the gift and the date of application.

For example, if you make a gift of $10,000 to a child and then apply for Medicaid within 36 months after the gift, you will be ineligible for Medicaid for about four months after the date of your gift ($10,000 ÷ $2,595 = 3.85 months). This means that if you applied for Medicaid immediately after you made the gift, then you will have to wait three to four months to qualify. If you applied for Medicaid more than four months after you made the gift, then the gift would not disqualify you from Medicaid assistance.

In addition to planning for the Medicaid transfer penalty, in making any gifts or transfers to children, you must take into account the gift, estate, and income tax consequences of such gifts, as well as your loss of control over the resources you give away.

14

ANATOMICAL GIFTS

One of the easiest ways to "work a miracle," as a brochure from the Oregon Donor Program puts it, and give the gift of life is to donate all or part of your body to medical science or for transplants. You can make this gift under the Uniform Anatomical Gifts Act which is in effect in every state.

a. WHO MAY BE A DONOR?

There are two ways to make anatomical gifts. First, you can make a gift of all or part of your body, to take effect at your death, by completing a document of gift. To do so, you must be capable of making health care decisions and be 18 years of age or older.

Second, if a family member has died, you can make an anatomical gift of all or part of the deceased family member's body. The deceased family member can be an adult or a minor, including a stillborn infant or fetus.

Persons who are authorized to donate a deceased person's body, in order of priority, are the deceased person's

(a) spouse,

(b) child 18 years of age or older,

(c) parent (either one),

(d) brother or sister 18 years of age or older,

(e) guardian, or

(f) next of kin.

The family members listed may not make a gift if an individual in a prior class is available to make the gift; the individual proposing to make the gift knows of a refusal or contrary indication by the deceased person; or the individual proposing to make the gift knows of an objection by another member of the individual's class or a member of a prior class.

b. HOW TO MAKE THE GIFT

There are four ways to document your intent to become an anatomical donor. Because of the importance of knowing that you are a donor immediately at your death, you may wish to use more than one, and perhaps all four ways.

1. Sign a donor card

Your signature need not be witnessed. However, if you cannot sign, the card must be signed by another individual and two witnesses, all of whom must sign at your direction and in your presence and in the presence of each other. Once you sign the card, you should carry it in your wallet.

You may get a donor card and other information about anatomical gifts from Oregon Donor Program. It is a public education coalition of six organizations promoting anatomical gifts: Lions Eyebank of Oregon, Oregon Eye Bank, Oregon Tissue Bank, Pacific Northwest Transplant Bank, Pacific Northwest Red Cross Blood Services, and whole Body Donation Program. Its address and telephone numbers are:

P.O. Box 532
Portland, Oregon 97207
1-800-452-1369 or 494-7888 in Portland

2. Sign a form at the Motor Vehicle Division

Sign a form at the Motor Vehicle Division, which will constitute a document of gift, and have your gift designated on your driver's license or identification card.

3. Make the gift in your will

If you do so, your anatomical gift is valid, even if your will is not admitted to probate or is declared invalid. However, a will may not be a practical way of making an anatomical gift, because your will may not be located and read until it is too late to carry out your wishes.

4. Make the gift in your advance directive

It is also a good idea to notify your family, clergy, doctor, and lawyer that you have made an anatomical gift. Make the gift in your advance directive and distribute copies.

c. HOW TO AMEND OR REVOKE THE GIFT

You may amend or revoke an anatomical gift by the following means:

(a) a signed statement;

(b) an oral statement made in the presence of two individuals;

(c) any form of communication during a terminal illness, addressed to a physician or surgeon;

(d) in the case of a gift made by driver's license or identification card application, lapse of the license, cancellation of the card, or by a statement made and delivered in the manner specified by the Department of Transportation;

(e) destruction, cancellation, or mutilation of the document of gift in the case of a gift not made by driver's license or identification card; and

(f) in the case of a gift made by will, amendment or revocation of the will.

An anatomical gift which you do not revoke before death is irrevocable and does not require the concurrence or consent of a family member or any other person after your death.

d. DUTIES OF PROCUREMENT ORGANIZATION

An organization authorized to accept an anatomical gift is known as a "procurement organization." The six organizations which are members of the Oregon Donor Program are the principal procurement organizations in Oregon.

A procurement organization may either accept or reject an anatomical gift. If the gift is of the entire body, then the organization may allow embalming and use of the body in funeral services. If the gift is of a part of the body, the organization shall cause the part to be removed without unnecessary mutilation.

If a person is in a hospital, is near death, and the person or the family has authorized an anatomical gift, then the hospital notifies the appropriate procurement organization. According to the Oregon Donor program, surgical removal of organs and tissues takes place either at a hospital or at a funeral home.

15
PROBATE ADMINISTRATION

Probate administration, or simply probate, as it is sometimes called, is a court-supervised procedure for settling the estate of a deceased person (known as the decedent) who dies owning probate property. Administration is not necessary for nonprobate property. (This distinction is explained in chapter 2.)

The purpose of probate is to settle all claims against the estate, whether by creditors or by heirs, and to transfer title to the probate property to the devisees if the decedent left a will, or to the heirs if the decedent died without a will. Generally, probate is necessary unless the estate is very small or if the decedent had only certain types of probate property. (See chapter 16.)

An Oregon probate court will have jurisdiction to probate all personal property located in Oregon or elsewhere. It also has jurisdiction to probate real property in Oregon. If the decedent had real property outside Oregon, a second or ancillary probate may be required. If the decedent was not a resident of Oregon, an Oregon probate court still has jurisdiction to probate any real property located in the state.

a. LOCATING THE WILL

The first step is to provide for funeral, burial, or other disposition of the body. Simultaneously, and equally as important, the family should determine if the decedent left a will. The most likely places for storing a will are the family home, the offices of the decedent's attorney, the decedent's safe deposit box, or the trust department of the decedent's bank. It is important to locate the most recent will.

Whoever has custody of a will must turn it over to the personal representative named in the will or the probate court within 30 days after receiving notice of the decedent's death.

There is no need to rush to the bank and try to close out the decedent's bank accounts before the state receives notice of the death. Oregon does not put a hold on or "freeze" bank accounts and safe deposit boxes when a person dies. If a bank account or safe deposit box is in the decedent's sole name, the personal representative can withdraw the funds in a bank account or remove the contents of a safe deposit box as soon as the probate court has appointed the personal representative. If a bank account or safe deposit box is owned jointly by the decedent and another person, the surviving joint owner can withdraw the funds or remove the contents immediately after the decedent's death.

b. WHO HANDLES THE PROBATE?

The person in charge of the probate is called the personal representative. The personal representative will be one or more persons named in the will. (If the person is named in the will, he or she is known as the executor (if male) or the executrix (if female).) If there is no will, the court will appoint a qualified person or bank. If there is no will, the person is called an administrator (if male) or an administratrix (if female).

The personal representative should retain an experienced probate attorney for assistance in administering the estate. Although the personal representative may, and often will, select the attorney who prepared the will, there is no legal requirement that this be done. The personal representative is free to select any attorney.

The personal representative and the attorney must decide on the division of functions between them. The attorney prepares and submits all documents that must be filed with the court. The personal representative, with the advice of the attorney, should locate and secure all property of the decedent, pay all claims, arrange for the sale of any property which is to be sold, communicate with beneficiaries, and arrange for final distribution to them. The more the personal representative can do, the less the attorney will have to do, and the less expensive administration should be.

The personal representative may also have to hire other professionals. An accountant may have to be retained for preparing income, inheritance, and gift tax returns if the attorney does not do this. The personal representative may also have to hire appraisers, real estate or stock brokers, or auctioneers to sell assets of the estate.

c. HOW TO START PROBATE PROCEEDINGS

Once it has been determined that probate administration is necessary, the next step is for the personal representative to file a petition for the court's approval of the appointment and, if there is a will, for proof of the will.

A will may be proved by the affidavits of the attesting witnesses swearing that they saw the decedent sign the will, they witnessed it in his or her presence, and, at the time, the decedent appeared to be of sound mind and over the age of 18 years. If the witnesses cannot be found and no affidavits were signed at the time the will was signed, then the will may be proved by testimony or other evidence of the genuineness of the decedent's signature or that of at least one of the witnesses.

When the original will cannot be found, proof may sometimes be made with a copy, if available, and by the affidavit or testimony of the will's drafter or witnesses.

d. PERSONAL REPRESENTATIVE'S BOND

A personal representative must file a surety bond with the court, unless —

- (a) the will provides that no bond is required,
- (b) the personal representative is the sole heir or devisee of the estate, or
- (c) all heirs and devisees agree in writing that the bond may be waived.

The purpose of the bond is to protect the beneficiaries and creditors of the estate from misconduct and mismanagement by the personal representative. The bond must be from a commercial surety company unless the court approves one or more personal sureties. The annual premium for a commercial surety bond is about $5 per $1,000 of assets, with a minimum premium of $100.

The amount of the bond is set by the court and need not equal the entire value of the assets. The court, in setting the bond, must look at the nature of the assets, their current value, the amount of expected income, and the probable indebtedness and taxes. The bond cannot be less than $1,000.

e. COURT APPOINTMENT OF THE PERSONAL REPRESENTATIVE

Once the court has appointed a personal representative and the bond, if necessary, has been filed, the court issues documents known as either Letters Testamentary (if a will has been admitted to probate) or Letters of Administration (where there is no will) certifying that the personal representative has been appointed. The personal representative then has authority to deal with the assets of the estate.

f. NOTICE TO HEIRS AND DEVISEES

Immediately after appointment, one of the first steps the personal representative must take is to send a required notice to all devisees and heirs. The notice must inform each heir and devisee of the name of the court and file number, the decedent's name and date of death, whether or not the will has been admitted to probate, the name and address of the personal representative and the attorney, the date of the personal representative's appointment, a statement advising the devisee or heir that his or her rights may be affected by the proceeding, and information as to where additional information can be obtained.

The personal representative must also send the required notice to any person who intends to contest the will, claim there is another will, or claim there was some agreement with the decedent concerning the will.

There is no requirement for a formal reading of the will by the attorney. Many people think this is required because they see it done on television shows. Although the will becomes a part of the probate court's record and is open to the public, the personal representative is not required to send a copy to the heirs and devisees. Normally, however, the personal representative either sends a copy of the will, or at least a description of it, to the heirs and devisees along with the required notice. As soon as the notices have been sent out, the personal representative should file an affidavit with the probate court reporting that the notices have been given.

g. NOTIFYING INTERESTED PERSONS

The personal representative must also immediately publish a notice in a newspaper of general circulation in the county where the probate proceeding is pending, known as "Notice to Interested Persons," informing the public in general of the title of the court, the name of the decedent, the name and address of the personal representative where claims may be presented, and a statement requiring anyone having claims against the estate to present claims within four months after first publication. The notice must appear in the newspaper once in each of three consecutive weeks.

h. LISTING THE PROPERTY

Within 60 days after being appointed, the personal representative must file an inventory, unless the court grants a longer time. The inventory must list all probate property of the decedent which has come into the personal representative's possession or knowledge, together with the personal representative's estimate of the true cash values of the assets as of the date of death.

Generally, the personal representative need not get accurate appraisals of all assets for purposes of probate administration. However, it may be necessary for the personal representative to get such appraisals for income and death tax purposes. If the personal representative seeks appraisals for those reasons, those values should also be used for the probate inventory.

i. WHAT THE PERSONAL REPRESENTATIVE DOES

The general duties of the personal representative are to collect the income from property of the estate and to preserve, settle, and distribute the estate in accordance with the terms of the will, or in accordance with Oregon law if there is no will, as expeditiously and with as little sacrifice of value as is reasonable under the circumstances.

Other duties include collecting assets of the decedent; paying claims, administration expenses, death taxes, or other income, gift or property taxes due; preserving and protecting the assets during the course of administration; and then distributing the assets to the persons entitled to them.

Generally, the personal representative is expected to proceed with administration, settlement, and distribution of the estate without court order. The attorney should counsel and assist the personal representative in each stage and prepare papers for filing with the court.

The personal representative has the general powers to carry out these obligations, including the power to sell, mortgage, lease, or otherwise deal with the property of the estate; to make investments of assets of the estate for limited purposes; to borrow money; to complete contracts of the decedent; and to continue any business or venture in which the decedent was engaged at his or her death.

j. CLAIMS AGAINST THE ESTATE

The personal representative has an affirmative duty to identify and notify persons who may have claims against the estate. During the first three months following appointment, the personal representative must make a reasonably diligent effort to investigate the financial records and affairs of the decedent to ascertain the names and addresses of possible claimants. The personal representative can get an extension of time to complete this search. Within 30 days after the end of this search period, the personal representative must give notice to each identified claimant whose claims have not been presented, accepted or paid in full. If a personal representative fails to give this notice, and a person who should have been notified files a claim after distribution has been made, the personal representative and any person receiving assets which should have gone to the claimant (whether heir, devisee, or another claimant) will have to pay the omitted claimant out of their own assets.

Generally, the personal representative pays all bills as they are presented, providing there are sufficient assets. He or she does not usually worry about the formalities of formal claims. However, the personal representative can insist on following the proper procedures, especially if the claim may be disputed or if the estate is insolvent. In such event, the person making the claim must present a written claim to the personal representative describing the nature and amount of the claim, the names and addresses of the claimants, and the attorney, if any. The claim must be presented to the personal representative at the address given in the notice to interested persons.

A claim is barred from payment unless it is presented within four months after date of first publication of notice to interested persons, or if the personal representative was required to give notice to a claimant, within 30 days after such notice. However, a claimant who does not receive actual notice of the probate must be paid to the extent of estate assets if the claim is filed before the final account and within two years after death.

Once a claim has been presented, it is considered allowed unless the personal representative mails or delivers notice of disallowance to the claimant and his or her attorney within 60 days after presentment. Thereafter, the disallowed claim is barred unless, within 30 days after mailing of the notice, the claimant either files a request for summary determination in the probate proceeding or begins a separate lawsuit against the personal representative.

If an estate is insolvent, the personal representative must make payment in the following order:

(a) Support for spouse and children up to one-half of the value of the estate, with periodic payments to continue for not more than one year after death

(b) The fees of the personal representative and the attorney and other expenses of administration

(c) Expenses of a "plain and decent" funeral and disposition of the remains

(d) Debts and taxes

(e) Reasonable and necessary hospital and medical expenses of last illness

(f) Certain state taxes

(g) Wages due employees of the decedent earned within 90 days before death

(h) Reimbursement for certain public assistance benefits

(i) All other claims

k. WHAT HAPPENS WHEN PROBATE IS DELAYED?

A simple probate administration should be completed within a year after a petition for probate is filed. There can be many reasons for delays beyond a one-year period, such as lawsuits involving the estate, delays in obtaining necessary tax clearances, and the necessity of completing sales of assets to have enough cash to pay claims and taxes.

Sometimes it is better for the beneficiaries and for the estate to keep the estate open beyond one year, especially for income tax purposes. However, sometimes the reason is simply attorney procrastination. The beneficiaries are entitled to regular reports on the status of the estate and when it can reasonably be expected that distribution will be made.

If there is going to be some delay in final distribution of all assets, it is possible to obtain a court order permitting a partial distribution. However, there must be sufficient assets left after distribution to pay support of the spouse and children, expenses of administration, and all unpaid claims.

If the estate is going to take longer than a year to probate, the personal representative must file an annual accounting within 30 days after the anniversary of his or her appointment reporting on the management of the estate.

l. FINAL ACCOUNT

When the personal representative is ready to make final distribution of the estate, he or she must file a final account with the court. If the estate is probated in less than a year, this will be the only accounting that must be filed with the court. There are two forms of an accounting: a detailed final account and a short form verified statement.

The short form verified statement is an expeditious way of closing an estate where all creditors have been paid in full and all heirs or devisees consent in writing to the short form procedure.

All the verified statement must say is that all creditors have been paid in full and all Oregon income and personal property taxes have been paid. It must be accompanied by a petition requesting the personal representative to distribute the property to the persons entitled to it as provided in the will, under the laws of intestate succession, or as agreed upon by the beneficiaries. It is not necessary to file any formal notice to the distributees nor is there any waiting period between the time for filing and the time for obtaining an order of distribution.

The formal final account requires a detailed accounting of all money and property received and all disbursements made, supported by canceled checks or other vouchers. It must also generally describe what the personal representative did during the course of administration. After the final account is filed, the personal representative must send to each heir and devisee, and to any creditors who have not received payment in full, notice that the final account has been filed and that such persons have not less than 20 days to file an objection to the accounting.

If any objections are filed, the court hears the objections. If no objections are filed, or if a short form verified statement has been filed, then the court enters a decree of final distribution, which approves the personal representative's administration of the estate, fixes fees for the personal representative and the attorneys, and directs distribution of the remaining assets of the estate to persons entitled to them.

After the court enters its decree of final distribution, the personal representative then distributes the property in accordance with that decree, gets appropriate receipts, and files the receipts or other proof of distribution, sometimes with a supplemental final account, with the court. The court then enters an order discharging the personal representative and closing the estate.

m. PAYING THE PERSONAL REPRESENTATIVE AND ATTORNEYS

The personal representative is entitled to a fee set by statute. The amount is calculated as a percentage of the whole estate, which is the value of the inventory, plus all income earned or gains realized during administration. The percentages (assuming an estate of $10,000 or more) are:

(a) $10,000 to $50,000: $430 plus 3% of excess over $10,000

(b) Over $50,000: $1,630 plus 2% of excess over $50,000

The personal representative is also entitled to a fee equal to 1% of the nonprobate property (other than life insurance proceeds). In addition, if extraordinary services have been performed by the personal representative, such as sale of real property, the personal representative is entitled to a fee for extraordinary services.

The attorney for the personal representative is also entitled to a fee that is fixed by the court. This fee is based primarily on the number of hours spent by the attorney, but also on factors such as the attorney's experience, the skill displayed, the results obtained, and the amount of responsibility assumed by the attorney.

n. RIGHTS OF THE SPOUSE AND DEPENDENT CHILDREN DURING PROBATE

Normally the family residence is owned jointly by husband and wife. In the unusual situation that it is not, and thus it becomes a probate asset, the surviving spouse and any dependent children of the decedent may continue to occupy the residence until one year after death. They have an obligation to keep the place in repair, keep it adequately insured, and pay all taxes and liens as they become due. Also, they must not permit any liens to attach to the property. If there is no surviving spouse, the dependent children still have the right to live there for one year after the death of the second parent. This does not require any court order.

A surviving spouse and dependent children are also entitled to support during probate. This may be done with a court order upon appropriate petition to the court. To determine the amount of support, the court considers the estate's solvency, the property available for support, and the property inherited by or devised to the spouse and children.

The court can provide support by transferring title to real or personal property or by periodic payments of money. However, the periodic payments cannot continue for more than two years after death. If the support payments would render the estate insolvent, support cannot exceed one-half of the value of the estate, nor can periodic payments continue for more than one year after death. Any support payments have priority over claims and expenses of administration and over any share for the distributees.

Finally, if it appears that reasonable provision for support of the spouse and minor children warrants that the whole estate (after payment of claims, taxes, and expenses of administration) be set apart for support, the court may do so four months after the notice to interested persons is published and then close the estate.

o. WHAT THE SURVIVING SPOUSE IS ENTITLED TO

Under Oregon's law of intestate succession, if you die without a will, your spouse is entitled to 50% of your probate property if there are children or other surviving issue of a prior marriage, or the entire estate if there are no such surviving issue or only issue of the present marriage. If you have a will, you may give your spouse less than the share of your estate to which he or she would be entitled without a will. However, you cannot totally disinherit your spouse. If you leave your spouse less than what he or she is entitled to, your spouse may elect to take the amount granted under Oregon law rather than what you left him or her in your will.

This "elective share" is equal to 25% of your probate property available for distribution. There is an additional limitation, however, requiring that nonprobate property be taken into account. This 25% will be reduced if the total of the elective share and nonprobate property received by your spouse exceeds 50% of the total probate and nonprobate property.

If the parties are not living together at the time of the death, the court has the discretion to deny the surviving spouse the right "to elect" against the will, depending on the circumstances, such as the length of the marriage, whether it was a first or subsequent marriage for either or both spouses, the contribution of the surviving spouse to the property of the decedent in the form of services or transfer of property, and the length and cause of separation.

To elect against the will, a surviving spouse must file a statement that he or she elects to take the elective share, and this must be done within 90 days after the date of admission of the will to probate or 30 days after the date of filing the probate inventory, whichever is later.

p. LIABILITIES OF A PERSONAL REPRESENTATIVE

A personal representative has the same duty of due care and loyalty to the heirs, devisees, and creditors of an estate that a trustee has to the beneficiaries of a trust. Specifically, a personal representative is liable for any loss caused to the estate arising from neglect in collecting assets of the estate or paying over money or delivering property of the estate; failure to pay taxes when due or to close the estate within a reasonable time; embezzlement or commingling of estate property; or any other wrongful act or omission.

If a personal representative breaches any of these duties, he or she can be removed, surcharged (i.e., required to pay damages), and denied compensation.

q. WILL CONTESTS

A person can contest a will or claim an interest in an estate if the person believes and can prove that the will admitted to probate is ineffective, for instance, because of lack of capacity or undue influence; that there is another will; or that the decedent agreed, promised, or represented that the decedent would make or revoke a will or devise, or not revoke a will or devise, or die intestate.

A will contest or similar claim must be filed within four months after notice from the personal representative, if the person was entitled to notice. Otherwise, the contest must be filed within four months after the first publication of notice to interested persons.

16
WHEN YOU LEAVE A SMALL ESTATE

Oregon has several methods of settling small estates and transferring probate property without formal probate administration. The principal vehicle is the small estate affidavit. In addition, some probate property may be transferred at the owner's death without probate provided that it is the only probate property.

a. THE SMALL ESTATE AFFIDAVIT

The small estate affidavit is a quick, inexpensive method of settling an estate when the property meets the qualifying limits. Also, there must be a consensus among the heirs and devisees on how to proceed, and there must be no disputed creditor's claims or other problems that might require a court order to settle.

1. Qualifying property

To qualify for the small estate affidavit, all the decedent's probate personal property must have a combined fair market value of $50,000 or less, and all the real property must have a combined fair market value of $90,000 or less. These are the limits for small estate affidavits filed after September 9, 1995. Before that date, the limits were $25,000 for personal property and $60,000 for real property.

2. The affidavit

The affidavit is signed by one or more "claiming successors" who are the devisees, heirs, or creditors of the estate. The affidavit must —

(a) state the name, age, domicile, post office address, and social security number of the decedent,

(b) state the date and place of decedent's death,

(c) describe all the probate property and list the fair market value,

(d) state that no personal representative has been appointed,

(e) state whether or not decedent left a will,

(f) list the names and addresses of the heirs and devisees and state that a copy of the affidavit and a copy of the will, if any, will be mailed or delivered to each heir and devisee,

(g) state the interest of each heir or devisee,

(h) state that reasonable efforts have been made to ascertain all creditors of the estate, list the name, address and amount due to each claimant, including disputed claims, and state that a copy of the affidavit will be mailed to each creditor,

(i) state that a copy of the affidavit will be mailed or delivered to Adult and Family Services Division, and

(j) state that any unlisted claims or claims for more than the amounts listed will be barred if not presented within four months and that disputed claims will be barred if a petition for summary determination is not filed within four months.

A certified copy of a death certificate and the original will, if any, must be attached to the affidavit.

The affidavit cannot be filed for 30 days after the death. It is filed with the county clerk as part of the probate records in the county where the decedent died, was domiciled, or resided at the time of death, or in the county where property is located at the time of death or when the affidavit is filed. The usual filing fee is $25.

Within 30 days after the affidavit has been filed, the claiming successor must mail a copy to each heir and devisee, to each creditor whose claim has not been paid or whose claim is disputed, and to the Adult and Family Services Division, Estate Administration Section.

If the decedent owned real property, the claiming successor must sign and record a claiming successor's deed in each county where the decedent's real property is situated.

Once ten days have elapsed after the affidavit has been filed, the claiming successors may submit a copy of the affidavit to anybody who has property belonging to the decedent or who owes the decedent money. Such persons are required to deliver the property or pay over the money to the claiming successor. This includes banks holding checking or savings accounts as well as companies in which the decedent owned stock.

The claiming successor must pay claims of creditors of the decedent presented within four months after filing the affidavit. If a personal representative is not appointed for the estate within that four-month period, then at the end of the four-month period, all the property belongs outright to the persons shown in the affidavit to be entitled to it, and any other claims against the property described in the affidavit are barred. However, it is important to make certain that all heirs or devisees are included in the affidavit; if not, they could later come back and claim their share of the property, even though they were not included in the affidavit.

If there is real property, the claiming successor will eventually want to sell that property and obtain title insurance for it. One disadvantage of the small estate affidavit is that a title insurance company may charge a higher premium than it would for insuring title if the property had gone through formal probate administration. Therefore, before you use a small estate affidavit to pass title to real property, it is advisable to check with a title insurance company to determine what would be required to ensure marketability of the title.

b. DEPOSITS WITH FINANCIAL INSTITUTIONS

If the only probate property is one or more accounts at a bank, savings and loan association, or credit union, an alternative to the small estate affidavit is to submit an affidavit to the financial institution where the funds are located and obtain release of the funds without formal probate administration. Here are the rules:

(a) The amount of funds on deposit in each type of financial institution (commercial bank, credit union, savings and loan association) cannot exceed $15,000 per type of institution. If there are three separate accounts of $15,000 each, one at a credit union, one at a savings and loan association, and one at a commercial bank, the full $45,000 could be released through this procedure.

(b) The persons entitled to the funds, in order of priority, are the surviving spouse, Adult and Family Services Division, to the extent of any public assistance received by the decedent, the surviving children 18 years of age or older, the surviving parents, and surviving brothers and sisters 18 years of age or older.

(c) The affidavit must state where and when the decedent died and that the total deposits in all such financial institutions in Oregon do not exceed $15,000. It must show the relationship to the decedent of the party making the affidavit and promise to pay the expenses of last illness, funeral expenses, and debts out of the funds on deposit to the full extent of the funds, if necessary, and to distribute any balance to the persons entitled to it.

(d) The financial institution will transfer the funds upon receipt of the affidavit. It is under no obligation to determine the relationship of the person making the affidavit to the decedent.

(e) The transfer of funds may be made without formal probate. However, if a personal representative is appointed, the person receiving the funds is required to account for them to the personal representative.

c. MOTOR VEHICLES

Title to motor vehicles in a deceased owner's sole name may be transferred without probate by filing with the Motor Vehicles Division an affidavit signed by all the heirs of the owner and stating the name of the person to whom ownership is to be transferred. If any heir has not reached majority or is incapacitated, a parent or guardian can sign the affidavit. The form of the affidavit is prepared by the Motor Vehicles Division. The Motor Vehicles Division will issue a new certificate and registration upon receipt of the old certificate of title, if any, the affidavit, and a registration fee.

d. WAGES

Any wages up to $3,000 earned by an employee from an employer other than the State of Oregon and unpaid at the employee's death must be paid to the employee's surviving spouse, or if there is none, to the employee's dependent children, or their guardians or conservator, in equal shares.

e. UNPAID MONEY

Any amounts up to $10,000 due a person from the State of Oregon, which are unpaid at the person's death, and any salary or wages due a deceased state employee of the State of Oregon, without limitation, may be distributed without a probate of the deceased person's estate if it is not in probate. The unpaid amount must be paid to the person's surviving spouse, or, if there is none, to the trustee of a revocable living trust created by the decedent, or, in order, to the decedent's children, parents, siblings, or nephews and nieces.

f. REAL PROPERTY

If the only probate property is a parcel of real property, it is possible to transfer title to the property and give good title to a buyer without formal probate. This would normally be done only if the property were worth more than $90,000 and the small estate affidavit could not be used. This technique is conditional upon a title insurance company being willing to insure title to the property. The following is required:

(a) There must be a sale of the property from the heirs or devisees to a third party.

(b) All heirs and devisees must be competent and willing to sign a deed or contract of sale.

(c) One or more of the heirs or devisees must submit an affidavit of heirship to the title insurance company and agree to indemnify the title insurance company against creditors' claims or claims of missing heirs.

The title insurance company will charge an additional "at risk" premium, which will usually be double the normal title insurance premium, unless the sale occurs many years after the death.

g. SAVINGS BONDS

Under federal regulation, savings bonds of a deceased sole owner may be redeemed without probate upon submission of proper forms.

For Series EE and HH bonds, if the face amount is under $500, the bonds will be paid to the person who has paid the burial expenses and who has not been reimbursed. If the amount does not exceed $1,000, and there is no will, the bonds may be paid to the survivors in the following order of preference:

(a) Spouse

(b) Children or other issue

(c) Parents

(d) Brothers and sisters

If the amount of the bonds is over $1,000, the proceeds may be paid to the heirs and devisees as they all agree.

h. OTHER ASSETS

There are certain assets, which do not have title documents, that may be transferred without probate administration. For instance, tangible personal property, such as furniture, stamp collections, and jewelry, do not have title documents and may be transferred without probate administration. Similarly, securities payable to bearer and not written to the order of a specific person can be transferred by delivery.

Generally, such transfers can be accomplished where there is family harmony. However, if the personal property has significant value (e.g., a valuable work of art, diamond ring, or antique), it may be necessary to go through probate to protect the property from claims of creditors and to determine who owns the property.

17

ESTATE AND INHERITANCE TAXES

Very few estates are now subject to estate or inheritance taxes. For most estates of decedents dying after December 31, 1986, there is no federal estate tax unless the estate is over $600,000. There is no Oregon Inheritance tax unless there is a federal estate tax to pay. The amount of the Oregon inheritance tax is based on a credit for state death taxes which may be deducted from the federal estate tax.

a. THE FEDERAL ESTATE TAX

The federal estate tax is calculated as follows:

(a) Calculate the gross estate

(b) Deduct all allowable deductions to get the taxable estate

(c) Add back in any taxable gifts made during the decedent's lifetime

(d) Calculate the tentative tax from the Unified Rate Schedule (see Table #1 at the end of this chapter).

(e) Deduct any gift taxes paid by the decedent to get the gross estate tax

(f) Deduct the unified credit of $192,800 (which is equivalent of a $600,000 exemption)

(g) If there is any tax due, deduct any credits, including the credit for state death taxes, to determine the balance due.

1. The gross estate

The gross estate consists of all property the decedent owned at death, plus certain property the decedent transferred during his or her life. It doesn't matter where the property is located, whether in one or more states or in another country, and it includes probate and nonprobate property. If the decedent owned only a partial interest in property, then only that partial interest is included in the gross estate.

Most property must be reported at its fair market value. Cash, life insurance proceeds, and the like are reported at face value. Publicly traded securities are listed at the mean between their high and low on the valuation date. Other kinds of property, such as real property and works of art, require an expert appraisal.

A personal representative may elect to value real property used for farms and closely held businesses on the basis of actual use rather than fair market value. This exception is intended to relieve the burden of death taxes on farmers and other small business people who traditionally are land rich and cash poor.

The entire gross estate is valued either at the date of death or at the alternate valuation date, which is six months after death. You must use one of the two dates for all assets and cannot pick and choose between the dates for different assets. The alternate valuation date might be used in a declining market if most of the assets were not to be sold right away. The value used for estate tax purposes fixes the basis for determining gain on later sale for capital gains income tax purposes. The alternate valuation date can be used only if its use reduces the amount of estate tax.

2. Probate property

Probate property owned in the decedent's name alone is listed on the federal estate return at full value. Property owned as tenants in common is listed with the fair market value of the decedent's portion.

The following kinds of probate property should be included:

(a) Real property, including property being bought on contract

(b) All stocks and bonds including savings bonds or other government securities

(c) Stock in the decedent's own corporation

(d) All notes, mortgages, and trust deeds being paid to the decedent

(e) All cash on hand

(f) Household goods, jewelry, royalty rights, remainders, judgments, and interest in a partnership

(g) Any other probate property

3. Joint and survivorship property

Property owned jointly with right of survivorship by the decedent and another person must be reported on the estate tax return at its full value. If the property was owned jointly by the decedent and a surviving spouse who is a U.S. citizen, then one-half of the value may be deducted.

A different rule applies for property owned jointly with right of survivorship by persons who are not married to each other or by a decedent and a surviving spouse who is not a U.S. citizen (even if the surviving spouse is a permanent resident of the United States). The full value of the jointly owned property must be included unless the surviving joint owner originally owned all or part of the property or furnished part of the consideration for its acquisition, or unless the two owners received the property jointly as an inheritance, devise, or gift from someone else. If the surviving joint owner cannot prove his or her contribution, then the full value must be listed.

4. Property transferred before death

Federal estate tax is imposed on certain transfers of property that the decedent made while still alive. The following information must be given on the tax return.

(a) Any federal gift taxes paid on gifts made during the three years before the death

(b) The full amount of the proceeds of any life insurance policy given away during the three years before the death

(c) The value of any property over which the decedent had a power of appointment if that power was relinquished during the three years before the death

(d) The value of any property transferred during the decedent's lifetime in which the decedent reserved a life estate

(e) Lifetime transfers that the decedent reserved the right to amend or revoke, such as assets in a revocable living trust

(f) Certain transfers to family members of business interests having a disproportionately large share of the potential appreciation where the decedent retained an interest in the income of the business. An example is if a person transfers common stock in a family corporation to a child, but retains the preferred stock. Generally, if a business grows, the common stock appreciates in value and the preferred stock does not. Under this rule, the common stock would be included in the person's estate, even though the person did not own it at death. This is the so-called "antifreeze" law.

5. Other nonprobate property

The full amount of the proceeds of all life insurance policies on the decedent's life which the decedent owned, or over which the decedent had "incidents of ownership" (such as the right to change beneficiaries) and the value of any property over which the decedent had a general power of appointment must be listed. For certain large retirement plans, there is an additional 15% tax on excess accumulations.

b. DEDUCTIONS

Deductions that can be made from the gross estate are —

(a) Funeral expenses

(b) Personal representative's fees

(c) Attorney fees and other administration expenses

(d) All unpaid income and property taxes, notes secured by a mortgage, and other debts

(e) Net losses during administration, such as losses from theft, fire, or storm not reimbursed by insurance

(f) Property passing to a surviving spouse who is a U.S. citizen. There is an unlimited marital deduction if the gift is not just an interest for life only. Property placed in special trusts for a surviving citizen spouse also qualifies for the marital deduction.

(g) Property for a surviving spouse who is not a U.S. citizen (even if the spouse is a U.S. resident), provided it is in a special trust, known as a "qualified domestic trust." Outright transfers to a noncitizen spouse, such as under a will, or nonprobate transfers, such as life insurance proceeds not in trust, do not qualify for the marital deduction.

(h) Gifts or irrevocable lifetime trusts to qualified charities

c. CALCULATING THE TAX

After deductions have been subtracted from the gross estate, add any lifetime gifts made by the decedent that required a gift tax return to be filed after December 31, 1976. Generally this will be any gift in excess of the annual exclusion ($3,000 per year before 1982 and $10,000 per year after 1981). With the new total, calculate the "tentative tax" from Table #1.

Next, deduct from the tentative tax due any gift taxes that the decedent paid for lifetime gifts and the unified credit of $192,800 (which is the equivalent exemption of $600,000). The federal gift and estate tax rates are unified in the sense that if a person makes lifetime taxable gifts (basically any gift worth more than $10,000 to one person in one year), any excess applies against the combined lifetime and death tax credit worth $600,000. This is why taxable gifts are added to the taxable estate and gift taxes paid are deducted from the tentative tax.

For instance, if a decedent had made a lifetime gift of $70,000 to one person, the decedent would have used $60,000 of the exemption equivalent (after deduction of the annual exclusion of $10,000), leaving $540,000 of the exemption equivalent for later lifetime gifts or as a credit against the estate tax. A person pays no gift tax until taxable gifts exceed the exemption equivalent of $600,000 (in which case there would be no credit left against the estate tax).

If there is a tax due after deduction of the unified credit, you may deduct a state death tax credit, which is either the amount of the state death tax or the maximum credit shown in Table #2, whichever is less.

Because Oregon imposes a tax equal to this credit, the estate of an Oregon decedent will always be able to deduct the maximum credit. There are several other credits against the estate tax, such as a credit for foreign death taxes and a credit for prior transfers, but they are rarely available.

If after deduction of all credits there is a tax due, it will have a marginal rate ranging from 37% to 55%. There is an additional 5% tax on estates between $10,000,000 and $21,040,000.

d. FILING THE RETURN AND PAYING THE TAX

An estate tax return (form 706) must be filed for every estate in which the gross estate exceeds $600,000. The return must be filed within nine months after death, but a reasonable extension may be obtained for good cause.

Any federal estate tax due must also be paid within nine months after death unless an extension of time to pay is obtained. An extension of time to file the return does not automatically extend the time to pay the tax. The IRS has the discretion to extend the time to pay for up to ten years after the due date for reasonable cause, such as lack of cash and inability to sell estate property except at a substantial loss to the estate. An estate, as a matter of right, may defer a portion of the estate tax for up to 14 years at 4% interest if the tax is on certain qualifying closely held businesses.

e. THE OREGON INHERITANCE TAX

For estates of decedents dying after December 31, 1986, Oregon has repealed its inheritance tax. In any estate on which a federal estate tax is due, however, Oregon still imposes an inheritance tax, called a "pick-up" tax, equal to the maximum federal state death tax credit. If the decedent leaves property subject to death tax in two or more states, the credit will be apportioned among the states, and Oregon will require payment of its proportionate share of the tax. The tax is due nine months after the death.

f. GENERATION-SKIPPING TRANSFER TAX

In addition to the federal estate tax, federal law also imposes a tax on transfers that skip a generation (e.g., a gift from a grandparent to a grandchild). The tax is a flat rate equal to the maximum estate and gift tax rate (currently 55%). There is a $1,000,000 per transferor exemption.

g. MARRIED COUPLES AND BYPASS TRUSTS

For married couples with taxable estates over $600,000, use of a bypass, or credit shelter, trust at the death of the spouse first to die can minimize or eliminate death taxes in both estates.

For example, suppose a married couple with a net worth of $1,200,000 have typical mom-and-pop wills leaving all their property to each other, then to their children after both have died. There would be no death taxes on the first death because of the unlimited marital deduction. However, death taxes on the surviving spouse's death on an estate of $1,200,000 would be $153,000.

Suppose instead that the couple provided, either in their wills or living trusts, that on the first death, $600,000 worth of assets would go into a trust for the surviving spouse. The trust would be for the surviving spouse's benefit during his or her lifetime, then go to the children after the surviving spouse's death. There will be no tax on the first spouse's death because the assets going into the trust are exempt under the first spouse's $600,000 exemption.

Upon the surviving spouse's death, the assets in the trust will not be taxed in the surviving spouse's estate because the surviving spouse does not have complete control over the assets. Those assets "bypass" the surviving spouse's estate for estate tax purposes. The other $600,000 of assets owned by the surviving spouse would be exempt under the surviving spouse's exemption. By making use of both $600,000 exemptions, the couple would save their children $153,000 in death taxes.

TABLE #1
UNIFIED RATE SCHEDULE

Column A	Column B	Column C	Column D
Taxable amount over	Taxable amount not over	Tax on amount in column A	Rate of tax on excess over amount in column A
			(Percent)
0	$10,000	0	18
$10,000	20,000	$1,800	20
20,000	40,000	3,800	22
40,000	60,000	8,200	24
60,000	80,000	13,000	26
80,000	100,000	18,200	28
100,000	150,000	23,800	30
150,000	250,000	38,800	32
250,000	500,000	70,800	34
500,000	750,000	155,800	37
750,000	1,000,000	248,300	39
1,000,000	1,250,000	345,800	41
1,250,000	1,500,000	448,300	43
1,500,000	2,000,000	555,800	45
2,000,000	2,500,000	780,000	49
2,500,000	3,000,000	1,025,800	53
3,000,000	–	1,290,800	55

An additonal 5% tax for a total marginal rate of 60% is levied on taxable amounts between $10,000,000 and $21,040,000.

TABLE #2
MAXIMUM CREDIT FOR STATE DEATH TAXES
(Based on federal adjusted taxable estate which is the federal taxable estate reduced by $60,000)

Column 1	Column 2	Column 3	Column 4
Adjusted taxable estate equal to or more than –	Adjusted taxable estate less than –	Credit on amount in column (1)	Rate of credit on estate over amount in column (1)
0	$40,000	0	None
$40,000	90,000	0	0.8
90,000	140,000	$400	1.6
140,000	240,000	1,200	2.4
240,000	440,000	3,600	3.2
440,000	640,000	10,000	4.0
640,000	840,000	18,000	4.8
840,000	1,040,000	27,600	5.6
1,040,000	1,540,000	38,800	6.4
1,540,000	2,040,000	70,800	7.2
2,040,000	2,540,000	106,800	8.0
2,540,000	3,040,000	146,800	8.8
3,040,000	3,540,000	190,800	9.6
3,540,000	4,040,000	238,800	10.4
4,040,000	5,040,000	290,800	11.2
5,040,000	6,040,000	402,800	12.0
6,040,000	7,040,000	522,800	12.8
7,040,000	8,040,000	650,800	13.6
8,040,000	9,040,000	786,800	14.4
9,040,000	10,040,000	930,800	15.2
10,040,000	–	1,082,800	16.0

18
GIFT TAXES DURING YOUR LIFETIME

a. THE FEDERAL GIFT TAX

Federal law imposes a tax on the lifetime transfer of any property that has monetary value from one person (the donor) to another person (the donee) for no consideration, or for consideration that is less than the value of the property given. There are four elements to a taxable gift:

(a) The donor and donee must be competent.

(b) The donor must intend to give up title and control of the property.

(c) There must be a voluntary irrevocable transfer or delivery of the property.

(d) The gifted property must be accepted by the donee.

1. Kinds of gifts

An outright gift might be cash, securities, or a house where title is transferred from the donor's name to the donee's sole name.

The creation of joint interest, such as a tenancy in common, can be a gift. If the donor conveys title to a house from the donor's sole name to the donee so they each own an undivided half as tenants in common, the donor has made a gift of one-half of the value of the property. If a donor conveys a remainder interest to the donee, reserving a life estate, the donor has made a gift of the value of the property less the actuarial value of the life estate.

A sale of property for less than fair market value is a bargain sale and is considered a gift. If you sell your house that is worth $75,000 to your daughter for $50,000, you have made a gift to her of $25,000. This rule does not apply when it is an arm's length sale to a non-relative.

If you set up an irrevocable lifetime trust and transfer property to the trustee, you have made a gift for tax purposes. This does not apply to transfers of a revocable trust since you have not given up control of the property.

An indirect gift might be paying off an obligation owed by someone else. However, under certain circumstances, paying medical expenses or tuition for someone else will not be considered a gift for tax purposes.

2. Reporting gifts

Gifts must be reported for gift tax purposes at fair market value at the date of the gift. Gifts of a partial interest in property are reported at the value of the partial interest. For instance, suppose a 50-year-old male made a gift of a remainder interest in a house worth $100,000, reserving a life estate, and the current federal rate was 8%. Based on actuarial tables, the value of the remainder interest, which would be reported for gift tax purposes, would be $17,697.

Gifts to qualified charities and gifts to a citizen spouse are 100% exempt from the gift tax. However, a gift to a citizen spouse that is limited or terminable, such as a life estate, does not qualify for the marital deduction. Gifts to a noncitizen spouse are excluded from the gift tax only up to $100,000 a year.

Taxable gifts mean the total amount of gifts made by a donor during a calendar year less —

(a) any charitable or marital deductions,

(b) amounts paid on behalf of certain individuals for educational and medical expenses, and

(c) an annual exclusion of $10,000 per donee.

There is no limit to the number of donees you may have. If you wanted to give $10,000 to each of five different persons in one year, for a total of $50,000, you would not have made a taxable gift because of the annual exclusion.

A husband and wife may split their gifts and use both their annual exclusions and their unified credits. For example, if a husband wants to make a gift of $20,000 of his own property, and his wife consents to the gift, the gift will be treated as having been given half by each spouse. If a husband and wife elect gift splitting, they become jointly liable for the gift tax for that calendar year.

To qualify for the annual exclusion, the gift must be of present interest and not a future interest. For example, a gift of a remainder interest in a house is a future interest. Because the gift tax is cumulative, the tax on gifts for the current year takes into account any taxable gifts made by the donor during the donor's entire life prior to that year.

As discussed in chapter 17, the federal gift and estate tax rates are unified. The gift tax for any given year is calculated by adding up all taxable gifts for the current and prior years, calculating the tax on the total taxable gifts for all years to date from the Unified Rate Schedule (see Table #1 in chapter 17), deducting the portion of the tax relating to taxable gifts for prior years, applying the unified credit of $192,800, then deducting any portion of the unified credit used for prior years. If the tax exceeds the unified credit, you pay the excess as gift tax. You do not pay gift tax unless the cumulative total of taxable gifts you have made during your lifetime exceeds $600,000, which is the exemption equivalent of the unified credit of $192,800.

You must file a gift tax return any year in which you make a gift of a present interest exceeding $10,000 in value to any one donee, or any year in which you make a gift of a future interest. You must file the gift tax return and pay any gift tax due by April 15 following the year of the gift.

b. THE OREGON GIFT TAX

Oregon has repealed its gift tax and does not impose a tax on lifetime voluntary transfers made after December 31, 1986.

APPENDIX
BANKS AUTHORIZED TO DO TRUST BUSINESS

Bank of America Oregon
121 S.W. Morrison, Suite 1700
Portland, OR 97204
Tel: (503) 275-1429

The Bank of California, N.A.
407 S.W. Broadway
Portland, OR 97208
Tel: (503) 225-2955

Bank of Commerce
P.O. Box 50
Milton-Freewater, OR 97862
Tel: (503) 938-5544

Columbia Trust Company
P.O. Box 1350
Portland, OR 97207
Tel: (503) 222-3600

The Commercial Bank
301 Church Street, N.E.
P.O. Box 428
Salem, OR 97308
Tel: (503) 399-2900

First Interstate Bank of Oregon, N.A.
1300 S.W. Fifth Avenue
P.O. Box 2971
Portland, OR 97208
Tel: (503) 225-3429

First Security Bank of Oregon
580 State Street
Salem, OR 97308
Tel: (503) 945-2358

First Security Bank of Utah, N.A.
580 State Street
Salem, OR 97308
Tel: (801) 246-6000

Key Trust Company of the Northwest
Head Office
200 Pacwest Center
1211 S.W. Fifth Avenue
Portland, OR 97204
Tel: (503) 790-7650

Pioneer Trust Company
109 Commercial Street, N.E.
P.O. Box 2305
Salem, OR 97308
Tel: (503) 363-3136

United States National Bank of Oregon
P.O. Box 8837
Portland, OR 97208
Tel: (503) 275-6588

U.S. Trust Company of the Pacific Northwest
4380 S.W. Macadam Avenue, Suite 450
Portland, OR 97201
Tel: (503) 228-2300

Western Bank
P.O. Box 1784
Medford, OR 97501
Tel: (503) 269-5171

West One Bank Oregon
234 S.W. Broadway
Portland, OR 97232
Tel: (503) 226-6666

West One Trust Company
P.O. Box 2882
Portland, OR 97204
Tel: (503) 273-5525

GLOSSARY

ADMINISTRATION

A court-supervised proceeding for transferring your property on your death. (See also **PROBATE ADMINISTRATION**.)

ADVANCE DIRECTIVE

Form which a person can sign naming health care representatives and directing how health care decisions are to be made for a person in case of a person's incapacity.

AGENCY ACCOUNT

A special form of deposit account with a financial institution, similar to a power of attorney.

ANCILLARY PROBATE

A second probate administration in another state. This commonly occurs when the decedent owns probate real property in more than one state.

ANNUITY

A contract providing for yearly (or monthly) payments.

ANTENUPTIAL AGREEMENT

See **PREMARITAL AGREEMENT**.

ANTILAPSE

Refers to the rule that determines who gets property given to a devisee under a will who predeceases the testator.

ATTESTATION CLAUSE

The clause signed by witnesses to a will.

ATTORNEY-IN-FACT

An agent authorized to act under a power of attorney; to be distinguished from an attorney at law, who is a person authorized to represent a party in a legal matter (a lawyer).

BENEFICIARY

(a) A person for whom a trust is established (See also **TRUST**.

(b) The recipient of life insurance proceeds.

(c) The recipient of property under a will.

BEQUEATH

To dispose of personal property in a will. This term is now archaic and is usually referred to as devise.

BEQUEST

A disposition of personal property by will; usually called a devise.

CERTIFICATION OF TRUST

A form, to be signed by a trustee of a trust, providing a summary of information about the trust and the trustee's authority.

CODICIL

An amendment to a will.

COMMUNITY PROPERTY

A form of property ownership between married persons under the laws of certain states other than Oregon. Oregon is known as a *common law* state.

CONSERVATORSHIP

A court-supervised legal proceeding to handle and protect the property and affairs of a minor or incapacitated person. The person appointed to handle the affairs is called a *conservator* (formerly called a *guardian of the estate*). The person for whom the conservatorship is set up is called the *protected person*.

CORPORATION

An artificial legal entity created by state law and used for conducting business.

CUSTODIANSHIP

A procedure, not supervised by the court, for managing property of minors. A *custodian* is the person handling the property.

DECEDENT

A person who has died leaving property subject to probate administration; more generally a deceased person.

DECLARATION FOR MENTAL HEALTH TREATMENT

A form which a person can sign directing how certain mental health decisions would be made for a person if a person becomes incapacitated.

DEED

A document by which you transfer or convey title to real property. The person conveying the property is called the *grantor*. The recipient of the property is called the *grantee*. For a conveyance of real property to be legally effective, the deed must be both signed by the grantor and delivered to the grantee. The deed should also be recorded. There are four types of deeds in Oregon, a quit claim deed, a bargain and sale deed, a warranty deed, and a special warranty deed.

DESCENT AND DISTRIBUTION

Another name for intestate succession.

DEVISE

To dispose of property by will (verb). A disposition of property by will (noun). There are three types of devises:

(a) Specific devise: A devise of a specific thing (e.g., rings or jewelry)

(b) General devise: A devise that is chargeable generally on your estate or property (e.g., a gift of $1,000).

(c) Residue: All probate property of an estate except property that constitutes a general or specific devise.

DEVISEE
A recipient of property under the will.

DIRECTIVE TO PHYSICIANS
A document by which you direct your physician not to use artificial means to keep you alive if you are terminally ill.

DISCLAIMER
A renunciation of a right to receive property whether under a will, trust, or other document.

DISINHERIT
To omit from your will a person who would have been an heir and would have received a share of your estate under the rules of intestate succession had you died without a will.

DISTRIBUTEE
A person entitled to property of a decedent either as a devisee under a will or, if there is no will, as an heir under intestate succession.

ESCHEAT
The rule of intestate succession that if a person dies without a will and with no heirs, all his or her probate property goes to the state.

ESTATE
All of a person's property or interest in property, real or personal. A person's probate estate is the person's probate

property. The *taxable* estate is all property subject to estate or inheritance tax.

ESTATE PLANNING

Planning the disposition of your property at death including preparation of a will, taking steps to minimize death taxes, and making certain all affairs and documents, such as title to property and designation of beneficiaries of life insurance policies, are in order.

EXECUTOR/EXECUTRIX

The names for a male or female personal representative named in the will.

EXORDIUM CLAUSE

The opening clause of a will.

FEE TITLE OR FEE SIMPLE

A form of ownership of real property in which only one person has any interest. This may be contrasted with a life estate, remainder interest, or tenancy by the entirety.

FIDUCIARY

A person who holds property in trust for another or who has a special relationship of trust to another. A personal representative, conservator, guardian, trustee, custodian and attorney in fact each stand in such a relationship.

GRANTEE

A person who receives a conveyance of real property.

GRANTOR

(a) A person who conveys title to real property by means of a deed.

(b) A person who sets up a trust; trustor.

GUARDIAN

A person appointed by a court and charged with the care and well-being of a minor or an incapacitated adult. The person for whom a guardian is appointed is called the protected person.

HEIR

Any person, including a surviving spouse, entitled under the laws of intestate succession to the probate property of a decedent who died wholly or partially intestate.

HOLOGRAPHIC WILL

A handwritten, unwitnessed will; not valid in Oregon.

INTANGIBLE PERSONAL PROPERTY

Stocks and bonds, bank accounts, life insurance, etc.

INTER VIVOS TRUST

A trust created and funded by a trustor while the trustor is still alive; also called a living trust.

INTESTATE

Without a will. A person dies intestate if he or she dies without a valid will.

INTESTATE SUCCESSION

The law that determines who will get your property on your death and who will be appointed the personal representative of your estate if you die with probate property and without a will.

IRREVOCABLE TRUST

A living trust in which the trustee gives up control of the property and cannot get it back.

ISSUE

See **LINEAL DESCENDANTS**.

JOINT ACCOUNT

A multiparty deposit account with a financial institution.

JOINT TENANCY/JOINT TENANCY WITH RIGHT OF SURVIVORSHIP

Two closely related forms of joint ownership of personal property with right of survivorship.

JOINT WILL/JOINT AND MUTUAL WILLS

Wills of a married couple contained in a single document; now rare.

LETTERS OF ADMINISTRATION

A court document certifying a person's appointment as an administrator or administratrix.

LETTERS TESTAMENTARY

A court document certifying a person's appointment as an executor or executrix.

LIFE ESTATE AND REMAINDER

A form of property ownership in which two or more persons have an interest in the property. The first person, the *life tenant*, is entitled to sole possession for life. Upon his or her death, the other person, the *remainderman*, has sole title and right to possession of the property.

LIMITED LIABILITY COMPANIES

A form of business entity which combines the limited liability protection of a corporation with the income tax treatment of a partnership.

LINEAL DESCENDANTS

Lineal descendants are a person's children, grandchildren, great-grandchildren, and any others who are in the same line of descent or subsequent generations. *Issue* has a more limited definition. It includes all lineal descendants except those who are lineal descendants of living descendants.

LIVING TRUST

A trust created and funded by a trustor while the trustor is still alive; also called an *inter vivos* trust.

LIVING WILL

See **DIRECTIVE TO PHYSICIANS.**

MINOR

In Oregon, generally an unmarried person under age 18.

MORTGAGE

A document given by the owner of real property to a lender or seller to secure payment of an obligation and to create a lien against the property. Similar to a trust deed.

NONPROBATE PROPERTY

Property not subject to probate administration.

NUNCUPATIVE WILL

An oral will later reduced to writing but not signed by the testator; not valid in Oregon.

PARTNERSHIP

An association of two or more persons to carry on a business for profit as co-owners. A partnership agreement may be written or oral.

PERSONAL PROPERTY

All property that is not real property.

PERSONAL REPRESENTATIVE

A person or financial institution appointed by a probate court to administer a decedent's estate.

(a) Executor/executrix: The title given a personal representative who is named in the decedent's will.

(b) Administrator/administratrix: The title given a personal representative if the decedent died without a will.

(c) Administrator/administratrix with will annexed: The title given a personal representative when the decedent dies with a will in which decedent fails to designate a personal representative or the personal representative is dead or otherwise fails to act.

(d) Administrator de bonis non: A successor personal representative.

POSTNUPTIAL AGREEMENT

An agreement between a married couple concerning their property and entered into after their marriage. It can also be called a marital property agreement.

POUR-OVER WILL

A will signed in conjunction with a living trust. The will provides that upon your death any probate property will be transferred to or "poured over" to the living trust.

POWER OF APPOINTMENT

A power granted in a trust to a person, called the donee or holder of the power, to direct who receives trust property.

POWER OF ATTORNEY

A document authorizing someone to act as your agent. That person is called your *attorney-in-fact*. You are the principal. A power of attorney may be general or limited. A power of attorney is *durable* if it is effective during the principal's incapacity. Generally a person will have one power of attorney for health care and a separate power of attorney for property and financial management.

PRECATORY

Language in a will that is a suggestion to your personal representative but is not legally binding on him or her.

PREMARITAL AGREEMENT

An agreement between a couple concerning their property and entered into before their marriage. Also called a prenuptial agreement or antenuptial agreement.

PRETERMITTED CHILD

A child inadvertently left out of your will.

PROBATE ADMINISTRATION

A court-supervised proceeding to transfer your probate property on your death from your name to the persons who are legally entitled to it, either under your will or pursuant to law.

PROPERTY

Anything of value or capable of being owned. All property may be categorized as follows:

- (a) Real property: Land and buildings or other fixtures permanently affixed to the land.
- (b) Personal property: All property that is not real property.
- (c) Tangible personal property: Furniture, clothing, motor vehicles, and the like.
- (d) Intangible personal property: Stocks and bonds, bank accounts, life insurance, contract rights, and the like.
- (e) Probate property: Property subject to probate administration.
- (f) Nonprobate property: Property not subject to probate administration.

REAL PROPERTY
Land and buildings on the land.

REMAINDER
(a) See **LIFE ESTATE**.

(b) Another word for residue.

REPRESENTATION
A rule determining which heirs inherit from a person dying intestate when the heirs are of unequal kinship.

RESIDUE
See **DEVISE**.

REVOCABLE TRUST
A form of living trust that the trustor may revoke during his or her lifetime.

SIBLING
A brother or sister.

SPECIFIC DEVISE
See **DEVISE**.

SPENDTHRIFT
A person who cannot manage his or her financial affairs and spends money extravagantly or wastefully.

SPOUSE
A husband or wife.

TENANCY BY THE ENTIRETY
Form of joint real property ownership by married persons.

TENANCY IN COMMON

A form of joint ownership involving two or more persons each owning an undivided interest, but with no right of survivorship. Each joint owner is called a *tenant in common*.

TESTAMENTARY CAPACITY

The mental capacity required to make, amend, or revoke a will.

TESTAMENTARY TRUST

A trust set up in a will or in the post-death part of a living trust and coming into effect after the death of the testator or trustor.

TESTIMONIUM CLAUSE

The clause in your will that states that you have signed it.

TESTATE

With a will. A person dies testate if he or she dies with a valid will. Otherwise he or she dies intestate.

TESTATOR

A man who makes a will.

TESTATRIX

A woman who makes a will.

TOTTEN TRUST

A form of bank account that you set up in your name as trustee for someone else, called the beneficiary, and is revocable while you are living.

TRUST

A trust is an arrangement in which one person known as the *grantor*, *settlor*, or *trustor* transfers property to another person or entity, known as the *trustee*, who administers the property for the benefit of some other person, known as the *beneficiary*. The trustor may be the beneficiary.

(a) Living (inter vivos) trust: A trust in which the trustor transfers property to the trustee while the trustor is still alive.

(b) Testamentary trust: A trust set up in a person's will or in the post-death portion of a person's living trust.

(c) Revocable trust: A form of living trust under which the trustor may terminate or revoke the trust during his or her lifetime.

(d) Standby trust: A form of revocable living trust.

(e) Irrevocable trust: A form of living trust under which the trustor cannot terminate or revoke. The trustor gives up all or most control of the property and cannot get it back.

(f) Sprinkling or spray trust: A trust under which the trustee is permitted to make unequal distributions to the beneficiaries.

TRUST ACCOUNT

A form of multi-party deposit account with a financial institution.

TRUST DEED

A document given by the owner of real property to a trustee in trust to secure payment of an obligation given by the grantor to a beneficiary. Similar to a mortgage and creating a lien against the property.

TRUSTOR

A person who transfers property in trust to another person.

TRUSTEE

Someone who administers property for another's benefit.

UNDUE INFLUENCE

Improper influence on a person making a will that invalidates the will.

WILL

A written declaration of a person's intentions concerning the disposition of his or her probate property at death.